# Growing Up on Maple Hill Farm

# Growing Up on Maple Hill Farm

## A New England Farm Life

By **Jerry Stelmok**

Voyageur Press

First published in 2007 by Voyageur Press, an imprint of MBI Publishing Company, Galtier Plaza, Suite 200, 380 Jackson Street, St. Paul, MN 55101 USA

Voyageur Press titles are also available at discounts in bulk quantity for industrial or sales-promotional use. For details write to Special Sales Manager at MBI Publishing Company, Galtier Plaza, Suite 200, 380 Jackson Street, St. Paul, MN 55101 USA.

To find out more about our books, join us online at www.voyageurpress.com.

Library of Congress Cataloging-in-Publication Data

Stelmok, Jerry.
  Growing up on Maple Hill Farm : a New England farm life / by Jerry Stelmok.
    p. cm.
  ISBN: 978-0-7603-2919-1 (hardbound w/ jacket)
  1. Stelmok, Jerry—Childhood and youth. 2. Stelmok, Jerry—Family. 3. Farm life—Maine—North Auburn Region—History—20th century. 4. Country life—Maine—North Auburn Region—History—20th century. 5. North Auburn Region (Me.)—Social life and customs—20th century. 6. Family farms—Maine—North Auburn Region—History—20th century. 7. Rural families—Maine—North Auburn Region—Biography. 8. North Auburn Region (Me.)—Biography. I. Title.
F29.N725S74 2007
974.1'82—dc22

2007017814

Edited by Dennis Pernu
Designed by Melissa Khaira

*Front cover: Approaching Storm*, by the author. *Frontispiece:* The author's cousin, Arnie Dickinson, in front of the Maple Hill hay barn, 1948. *Back cover:* The view from Maple Hill after Maine's 1998 ice storm.

Printed in the United States

For my parents,
Anthony (August 16, 1925–October 20, 2005) and Helen Stelmok.
Through love and good humor they put any hardships
in perspective and never forgot how to laugh and enjoy life.

# Contents

# ACKNOWLEDGMENTS

I wish to thank my acquisitions editor, Dennis Pernu, first for his support guiding this project through to publication, and second for his suggestions and careful editing of the material.

I am also grateful to Andrea Myers for transcribing my handwritten manuscript onto a useable disc, and to Todd Watts for doing essentially the same thing with my watercolor illustrations. Without friends like these, this story couldn't have made it out of Atkinson, Maine. Thank you, each of you.

# Introduction

My grandfather, Vincent Josef Stelmok, was born in a little village outside Vilnius, in the small but proud Baltic state of Lithuania in 1888. During that same year in Auburn, Maine, on a windswept hilltop variously called Maple or Dillingham Hill, a farmer by the name of Osgood completed the building of a barn on his two-hundred-acre farm. The post-and-beam structure was a hundred feet long and consisted of five twenty-foot bays. It had a dairy cow tie-up, box stalls, an inside silo, mows, scaffolds, and a cypress wood cistern kept full of sweet water that a windmill provided from a seemingly inexhaustible spring a quarter-mile across a field.

The barn was connected to the newly built two-story ell on the farmhouse by an enclosed shed. Prior to building the barn, Osgood had completed the transformation of the original cape on the property into a larger house of two full stories and a finished attic. In the center hall a pair of stairways with hardwood banisters and turned newel posts rose to the second and then third stories, and outside an elegant screened-in porch supported by graceful wooden columns afforded a perfect refuge in which to relax on warm summer evenings.

The original cape, constructed of splendidly hand-hewn beams and wide pumpkin pine boards probably cut from the property, had been built by Isaac Dillingham in 1797, according to Helen McIntosh, a summer resident along with her husband in a cottage just up the road from the farm. Mrs. McIntosh, herself a Dillingham, was a teacher and an amateur historian, and her father had once been the master of a little one-room school located on the hill. According to her, Isaac was the son of John Dillingham, who had built the first log cabin on the hill in 1783, just up the road from her cottage. The spot on which this cabin sat is commemorated by a bronze plaque affixed to a boulder. John and his father, Jeremiah Dillingham, were veterans of the Continental Army (Jeremiah was a veteran of the French and Indian War as well), and for their service during the Revolutionary War they were given land that included most of the hill in what was at the time part of the Commonwealth of Massachusetts. It's a small wonder descendents of John and Jeremiah always referred to the hill as Dillingham Hill, eschewing the more common Maple Hill most other residents favored.

Back in Europe in 1909, my grandfather, Vincent, then twenty-one, joined the mass exodus of refugees from the Baltic region, who were fleeing the tyranny of the Russian Czar and likely conscription into the Russian Army, recently depleted by a senseless and costly war with Japan.

Vincent fled to Germany and from Bremen booked passage to New York on the passenger ship *Breslau*. (In 1917 the ship was seized by the U.S. government, recommissioned the *Bridgeport*, and used during World War II as a troop transport and hospital ship.) Vincent disembarked at Ellis Island on April 23 and used his middle name, Josef. His last place of residence, Kuršenia, was recorded by officials as Krewzany, Russia!

After a year or two spent as a worker in a New Hampshire quarry, Vincent relocated to the mill town of Lewiston, Maine, where he had relatives. He worked as a weaver in a textile mill, met and married a fellow Lithuanian, Margaret Mason, who had come to America with her mother and three sisters. The couple soon started a family and in his spare time Vincent began fixing up houses and reselling them. In a few years he had enough rental income to quit his job at the mill. His new lifestyle, spending days at the Lithuanian club, playing cards, smoking, and drinking, soon began eroding his naturally robust health. Accordingly, he took a doctor's advice seriously, sold his in-town property, and purchased the showplace farm from the Osgoods, including its small herd of dairy cows. He and Margaret moved out to their new farm on the hill around the lake in November 1925. With them were their six children ranging in ages from fifteen down to the youngest, my father, Anthony, who was just three months old.

# CHAPTER ONE

## TONY'S STORY

My father's stories of growing up on Maple Hill Farm always seemed to me larger than life. They were more interesting, funnier, and sadder than anything I was experiencing when he related them to me. The way he told it, life was tougher, the winters colder, the summers hotter; yet, at the same time, neighbors were kinder, dogs were smarter, and life for the most part was better than the current situation. In relating these stories Dad painted from an impressionist's rich palette, and as I listened, transfixed, I imagined a world bathed in a celestial light.

At just three months of age, Dad missed a chance at an easier life when his parents left behind a successful property management business in town to take over a two-hundred-acre working farm on the hill around the lake. Being city folk—even back in Lithuania, where they emigrated from—they were ill-prepared to manage such an endeavor, especially moving in as they did on the cusp of a Maine winter. During their first week in their new homestead, the plumbing in the Victorian bathroom froze solid and the pipes burst, rendering its comforts useless. Rather than deal with it, my grandfather chose instead to make do with the outhouse connected to the back shed—a practice he continued for the next forty years.

Maple Hill Farm was a showpiece when the Osgood family turned it over to my grandparents, Vincent and Margaret, but by the time I was born twenty-five years later it presented quite a different aspect. By then the buildings were considerably weather-beaten, the porch sagging, roofs leaking, and the hundred-foot barn slumping. And although Gran'pa had been able to purchase the farm with cash after selling his real estate interests in Lewiston and Auburn, by the time he retired the farm was deeply in hock and presented Dad with a major challenge just to rescue the operation from collapsing.

None of this was necessarily Gran'pa's fault. He tried his best and picked up many skills rapidly. Still, upon his doctor's recommendation, he had embarked upon a career for which he was ill-prepared and had little natural talent.

16

With a large family to support and the nation's economy about to be clobbered by the Great Depression, it was a miracle he was able to hold onto the farm at all.

Dad's earliest memory—he must have been two—was of John, his elder brother, and Gran'pa fighting—physically—on the front hallway stairs. It was on a Sunday and Gran'pa had some fieldwork lined up for the older children. "Johnny" had other ideas, which included spending the afternoon in town. He was wearing his good suit and wasn't about to change his plans. The argument soon turned into a shouting match, and after the son declared he was not anyone's slave, and wasn't going to work seven days a week, the disagreement escalated to wrestling. It ended with Johnny, then sixteen, leaving home and vowing to make his own way in the world, and Gran'pa losing his best unpaid farmhand.

Within months Johnny was back on the hill as a hand on neighbor Frank Longel's farm. Longel had first checked with Gran'pa to see if that arrangement was okay with him. The next winter he was cutting wood for Longel, paid by the cord, and living back home, paying board. Uncle Johnny apparently had a hot temper, and when his boss suggested he might pile his cordwood a bit tighter he blew up and stalked off that job as well. Gran'pa got his short-fused son back on track by taking him, along with a bottle of whiskey, to the Bate's textile mill, where Gran'pa had once worked. He knew a foreman there and before they left—minus the whiskey—Johnny had been hired and was soon trained as a weaver. It was a trade he worked at until he retired, except for a hitch in the Navy during World War II. Uncle Johnny and his wife, Vula, lived on a small farm on the next ridge over from Maple Hill.

Hard work played a big role in the early years of all the Stelmok children of that generation. As soon as you were old enough to get around, you might as well be pulling weeds or picking beans. By the time you were eight or nine you could take care of the young stock, stack and carry in firewood. The herd was quite small then, and when the cows were let out to eat grass alongside a field planted in corn or beans, there was no reason to put up fencing when there were youngsters to watch the cows and chase them away from the tempting crops. This applied to the daughters—my aunts Anne, Lydia, and Helen—as well as to Dad and his older brother, Frank. Gran'pa was steering the operation toward raising vegetable crops and away from dairying. He never cared much for the cows—and Gran'pa knew lots of folks in town, and could peddle about anything.

I never knew my grandmother, Margaret. She died before I was born. The stories about her lead me to believe she was a strong, capable, and compassionate woman. From the start she was better around the cows than her husband, and as a result did all the milking; never mind she had five children at home, the youngest, my father, just an infant. Her cooking was legendary. As the children grew, everyone working harder, the family consumed prodigious amounts of food. Margaret would bake eight pies at a go, only to see them disappear in a day or two. She killed, cleaned, plucked, and cooked countless chickens, and always kept enough pullets to not only keep the family in eggs, but also to have dozens to sell to customers each week.

She was kind and warm-hearted and the neighbors all liked her. Winter evenings, when she'd finished her long day of work, she enjoyed sitting next to the warm floor register, and neighbors would often pay a call. Some, like Harold Johnson, liked playing checkers with her. He'd take the shortest path between the two farms by skiing across the fields in the moonlight, play until late into the evening, losing most of the matches, then bundle up and ski back home. Margaret was a huge comfort and source of advice to my mother, who was new to marriage, country life, and, when my sister Linda was born, motherhood. My grandmother was only fifty-nine when a heart attack took her, and it's not hard to believe she may have worked herself to death.

As the two remaining boys, Dad and his brother Frank, grew older, they could handle all the work piled upon them. The hardship made them close friends as well as brothers, and both of them were tough as nails. Frankie saw dairying as the best course for the farm's future, and this put him at loggerheads with his father, who favored raising vegetable crops. This led to an uneasy tension between Gran'pa and Frankie, with Dad agreeing with his brother, but too young to have a voice in the decision. As a result, the two directions were in competition and began undermining each other and robbing each other's space and energy.

This dualism also amounted to a lot more work. Now, besides milking and caring for the cattle, fencing, putting up loose hay, and winter woods work, there was plowing, weeding, cultivating. And picking vegetables. All the heavy work was powered by draft horses. Sweet corn became a major crop. Before the boys could begin cutting or hauling hay on a hot July day they first had to pick a hundred dozen or more ears of corn for Gran'pa's customers. On two blistering August days they filled an order for a thousand dozen ears—picked, bagged, and stacked inside a waiting trailer.

My aunts Lydia and Helen, and for a few years Annie, were out there in the fields with them, and the Stelmok sisters could outwork a lot of men. During high school the girls boarded with families in town, there being no regular transportation.

*A family portrait from 1961 at Aunt Helen Dickinson's house down the road. From left: Gran'pa Vincent, Aunt Helen, Mother, Dad (seated), me (with the big ears), Cousin Mike, Linda, Dad's Aunt Nellie from California, Aunt Annie, and Aunt Lydia.*

Like her brother, John, Annie couldn't escape the farm fast enough, and after graduation traveled to Massachusetts to visit relatives, and from there set off to see some of the country. She would return years later and spend the last twenty years of her life on the farm, downstairs with Gran'pa and Aunt Lydia.

Aunt Lydia loved farm life, including the work, and would happily have stayed on to help after high school. But Gran'pa didn't believe that farming was a proper career choice for a young woman and would not allow it. Lydia took a job in town at a mill, but missed the farm dearly. Once she bought an automobile, she moved back home, keeping her day job, but helping out with picking and packing the vegetables for market. She never married.

Aunt Helen, youngest sibling to Dad, also liked farm life, but she fell in love and married right out of high school. Helen and her family lived in the house across the road from Avery and Bessie Longel just down the road. Thus, Helen and her husband, Arnold, and their boys, our cousins Arnie and Mike, were always an integral part of our lives.

In winter Frankie worked in the woods, Dad helping his brother after school, before they shared the milking. For years, before dependable refrigeration was available, ice needed to be harvested from the lake and stored in a small icehouse around the back. By late February Lake Auburn would be imprisoned by a layer of clear ice at least two feet thick.

*Cousin "Arnie" Dickinson, me, and Linda in 1948. Aunt Helen, Arnold Sr.,
and cousins Arnie and Mike lived just down the road and were a big part of our
extended family. Arnie worked in the garden and haying for Dad and Gran'pa until
he was old enough to get official summer jobs that paid better.*

Once any snow cover was pushed off a patch, a checkerboard pattern of two-foot squares was scored deeply into the surface by a horse-drawn scriber. An initial block was sacrificed by laboriously chiseling it away. Then a long, coarse-toothed saw could be employed to cut a tier free. If conditions were right the hundred and fifty pound blocks could then be cleaved off with a few strikes from a chisel along the surface scores. The floating blocks were guided to a landing shelf where they were pulled out of the water and pushed up ramps onto a modified scoot or onto the bed of a truck. The implements used were a long-handled pick-like tool called an ice hook, and tongs.

Back at the farm the blocks were slid off the scoot and stacked in layers in the icehouse with sawdust applied for insulation. During the warm weather months, individual blocks would be removed from the storage shed and trundled on a dolly around to the milkhouse. There, the sawdust was scraped or hosed off and the block added to the cold water in the galvanized cooler that held the milk cans.

Cousins from town would come out to the farm during the summer to help with some of this work, especially during the Depression. Their only pay was a bed to sleep in and all the fresh, delicious food they could eat—which was not always guaranteed at their homes in town.

Youth being indomitable, even all this work wasn't enough to keep the two brothers from having some fun. During the long summer evenings after chores, Dad and Frankie might drive or walk a couple miles down to North Auburn village to play baseball on the local team. They might go even if no game was scheduled, just to hang out at the store, a gathering place to horse around, drink soda, and perhaps listen to a boxing match on the store's radio, especially if heavyweight champion Joe Louis was scheduled to defend his crown.

Both Frankie and Dad loved boxing, and they frequently went at it in the hay barn, using two pair each of work gloves for their mitts. These matches could get quite competitive, and both brothers suffered their shares of bloody noses, bruises, and contusions. One time Frankie launched a roundhouse left, which Dad ducked beneath and countered with a right that took his brother, still off balance and his torso twisted, right above the kidney. Frankie went down in a heap in severe pain and needed to be carried into the house. As a reward, Dad got to do his brother's chores along with his own for several days until the inflamed muscles had a chance to relax and mend.

This, however, did not spell the end of Frankie's boxing. Once he had his own car, he joined a gym in town and for a few years was a respectable amateur fighter locally, his fitness training being mostly work on the farm and in the woods. Dad often told me that his older brother might have been a notable boxer if he had trained more seriously and quit smoking.

The North Auburn store remained a hub of quiet sociability even in winter, and the brothers went there a couple evenings a week, even when it meant walking in near-zero temperatures. At times, especially in early winter, the conditions might be just right for ice-skating, a popular activity. Dad loved to skate, and his accounts of dozens of skaters gliding over the ice under a winter moon with a roaring bonfire burning on the shore, evoked images depicted on nineteenth-century Currier & Ives prints.

Dad's interest in hunting was something he developed by himself, under the influence and parsimonious advice of Clarence Johnson, a flinty Yankee subsistence farmer on the other side of the hill. Gran'pa had no interest in such pastimes and no inclination to take them up. It was his mother, Margaret, who took Dad at age thirteen to Montgomery Ward in Lewiston to purchase his first firearm: a Stevens .22 single-shot, bolt-action rifle. With it, Dad learned to shoot accurately and no doubt killed his share of innocent birds and squirrels in the process. Gradually, he also learned to stalk and sometimes shoot snowshoe hares that had turned partially white before snow had fallen, and grouse that were slow to take wing.

Old man Johnson was also a skilled trapper, and you had to be skilled to fool the wary foxes of central Maine in those days. By following Johnson's examples as best he could, Dad started trapping at fifteen, gleaning what information he could get from magazines, and the snippets of advice his reluctant mentor would let slip. It took him almost two seasons to catch his first fox, but once he'd figured it out, he became reasonably successful. Foxes were plentiful at the time, and good pelts worth a lot of money right up through the war. Even the few dollars paid for the easier-to-catch skunks and raccoons were a big help to a high schooler maintaining his own car. In one of his sets he once caught a beautiful silver fox with a coat of long black hair, rippled by white-tipped guard hairs. It was an escapee from the Longel's brief fox-raising enterprise and Dad took the unhurt and very valuable creature from the trap alive and returned it to his grateful neighbors.

Six years older than Dad, Frankie's interests started running along more mature lines long before his brother's. Increasingly,

Frankie would be off with his older friends on dates, often at dances around the area. Dad was good-looking and appeared older than his actual age, but not old enough at fifteen to interest women in their twenties. By all accounts Frankie was quite a ladies' man, and although he smoked cigarettes from an early age, he never took a drink.

With continued friction with Gran'pa on the farm, Frankie teamed up with a local woods operator and did well in the local logging business. In so doing, he sacrificed any possible deferment opportunities his work on the farm might provide. But that was all the same to him. He needed his independence. Eventually the inevitable draft notice came around and Frankie was inducted into the Army in 1944. Brother Johnny had by then been serving in the Navy for some time.

As Dad approached his senior year there was little doubt about what a strapping young man like him would be doing once he was handed his diploma in 1943: he'd either be enlisting or drafted into a branch of the armed services. That was fine with him. Defeating the forces of Hitler and the Japanese emperor were the top priorities of most Americans, and besides, Dad had really never been away from home and the farm, and this would give him that chance.

He hadn't planned on meeting a slight, pretty girl at a dance at the Crowley Junction Grange Hall who enjoyed dancing as much as he did. Helen Klimek was the daughter of

Polish immigrants who lived in Lewiston; and she was immediately struck by the tall, handsome, and considerate young man. They fell in love and began seeing one another every chance they got, which was about as often as Dad had any of the tightly rationed gasoline to spare. On August 19, 1944, the two were married at St. Patrick's Catholic Church in Lewiston. Frankie wasn't at the wedding because he was finishing up his military training and was expecting his unit to be mobilized to Europe in early winter. The war was going so well for the Allies in Europe at the time that everyone was hoping he might not have to go.

After a short honeymoon at Old Orchard Beach the young couple moved into the spare apartment Dad had fixed up in the second floor of the farmhouse. It was a shock to Mother, who was used to her parents' much nicer apartment in town and was a city girl at heart. There were lots of adjustments to be worked out and their deep love for one another helped them through some early difficult times.

When Dad received his draft notice, Gran'pa scheduled a hearing with the draft board, against his son's wishes. He explained to the board that with his two other sons now serving their country, the farm couldn't operate without my father, which was basically true. Dad never got a second notice directing him to report for induction.

On December 24, 1944, the troop ship on which

Frankie had sailed to Europe was torpedoed as it sat at anchor in a French harbor in the English Channel. Most of the ship's officers were ashore for the holiday celebrations, and although there was over an hour to tow the ship to shore before it sank, there was no one aboard who could initiate such a plan. When the USS *Leopoldville* finally went down, Private Frank Stelmok was one of several hundred soldiers aboard who lost their lives that Christmas Eve.

Everyone took the news very hard. Frankie was a good-natured and likeable young man with lots of friends. But most affected of all were Dad and his mother, Margaret. She never really got over the sorrow, and her son's death seemed to mark a steady decline in her health. A broken heart was a major factor in her death at fifty-nine.

With the certainty that Frankie wouldn't be returning to help run the farm, and with a child to support, Dad faced up to the reality that he was the one who was now charged with getting the farm on its feet and working, as best he could, around Gran'pa's old-fashioned ideas, to bring the operation into the twentieth century. Along that difficult path, he and Mother, through love and good humor, fooled Linda and me into thinking we were living the good life— and in many ways, that's exactly what we were doing.

# CHAPTER TWO

## WHEN I WAS VERY YOUNG

It's impossible to say for sure just what is my earliest memory of life on the farm, but I am quite certain that I remember my crib up against the wall in a small room that for a time was Dad's den. I remember a dark wallpaper, possibly burgundy, decorated with large flowers and sunlight streaming through the window that took up much of one end wall. The south-facing window overlooked the front yard that was partially encircled by the house, ell, shed, and the towering end of the barn. I'm standing, supporting myself by gripping the vertical slats of the adjustable side, the upper rail about even with my chin.

I remember the wind that slammed into the farmhouse set atop the hill, open to any assault from a northerly direction.

In winter the wind whistled down the tall chimneys, rushed along beneath the eaves like an auger, and rattled the loose panes of the windows that were coated by an arabesque tracery of thick frost. Of course, this wind-awareness might have come later in my life.

Try as they might, the probing fingers of the north wind never succeeded in penetrating the core of our upstairs apartment. Downstairs, where my grandfather and aunts Annie and Lydia resided, was heated primarily by a behemoth wood-burner furnace in the cellar, which sent its considerable volume of dry heat up through a single square floor register that was surrounded by a collection of accommodating chairs of all types. As kids, soaked from playing outside in the snow, we were never discouraged from standing on that intense heat source, our snow pants and mittens steaming, and melting clots of slush sizzling on the grate as they fell from our rubber boots.

Upstairs, on the other hand, was heated by a kerosene pot burner whose pipe was fitted with a hinged automatic damper that ticked softly and incessantly. Located in the living room, the earliest version I recall had a brown rounded sheet-metal cowling that was perforated by slots of all descriptions, in geometric patterns designed to allow the heat to escape into the room. A tame orange flame burned steadily in the depths of the heater, visible behind a tempered glass window.

The kitchen, located oddly enough on the vulnerable northwest corner of the uninsulated house, was heated by a wood-burning end heater attached to the gas range. Split wood and billets of small diameter were fed through round lids on the cast iron top surface. This small heater was worked hard throughout the winter and even so, during sustained cold spells it frequently fell short of keeping the water from freezing in the galvanized pipes that led up from below to our shallow iron sink.

Whenever Dad opened the flue damper and lifted one of the round lids to add firewood, bright hungry tongues of flame would leap upward in anticipation of this new infusion. The draft rushing up inside the tall chimney was seldom feeble, and whenever new chunks of birch or maple were introduced into the firebox a small inferno would flare, complete with smoke, flying sparks, and pulsating embers. Not infrequently, a chunk would be too large to drop comfortably into the box, forcing Dad to lift the second lid and the fitted connector between them. Cursing, he would jab at the stubborn chunk with the lid lifter until it settled into its fiery berth. Then the lids were dropped back in place and eventually the roar in the flue would abate, followed by a ticking and popping in the dull black stovepipe as the sheet metal contracted.

All of this was not without some anxiety, especially on Mother's part, and this nervousness was not lost on my sister

Linda and me. Fear of a catastrophic house or barn fire was one fear that persisted throughout my childhood, and it was not totally unfounded. I remember being hastily bundled into winter coat and hat by my distraught mother and sent down the back-shed stairs to wait out a roaring chimney fire in safety. A glance back just before closing the door, revealed a glimpse of Mother in a panic, splashing a dishpan of cold water onto the plaster wall that stood against the chimney that had become too hot to touch. The fire raging in the flue sounded like the roar of an approaching train.

Once outside in the yard, the seriousness of the situation was immediately evident by the thick column of dense yellow-brown smoke, flames licking at its base, that rolled briefly skyward from the chimney before being dispersed by the biting wind. Downdrafts caused by the surrounding structures drew enough of the sooty acrid smoke down into the yard to sting the eyes and fill the sinuses.

High up on the roof there was a permanent wooden platform spanning the ridge adjacent to the chimney, and on it perched Gran'pa, scooched low to avoid the brunt of the heat and smoke pouring forth, and waiting nervously as Dad ascended the two wooden ladders that were always in place for these not uncommon emergencies. A pail of water sloshed in his right hand, hopefully to slow down the blaze until the fire trucks arrived. On more than one occasion, these initial efforts were credited by the firemen with possibly saving the farmhouse.

But not all my early impressions are that exciting. Tamer ones include hot summer afternoons spent in the shade of the spreading maples and playing on the spacious front porch that was already beginning to sag away from the main house. This was a proper porch, with a granite step up and thick, capped half walls around the perimeter, sheathed on the inside, like the floor and ceiling, with beaded fir paneling, and on the exterior with weathered clapboards, beginning to lose their grip.

From the wide wooden cap, hollow, tapered wooden columns with bases and capitals rose to support the roof. Around the periphery, neglected flowerbeds, except for the daylilies, were overwhelmed by lacey asparagus, a swelling lilac bush, and clumps of knotweed waiting their chance to bolt and spread. All this added to a sense of privacy. When Dad was a boy the porch was fitted with removable screen panels, but by this time they had disappeared. But the open space still offered a keen sense of shelter during a downpour, and a refuge from the broiling sun, as, too young for real work, we played and waited for the clip-clop of the horses' hooves on the road and the appearance of the iron-wheeled wagon, piled high with a well-built load of loose hay. Dad, reins in hand, his copper skin standing out from a white T-shirt, stood high above the horses, Buck and Don, a straw of hay between his teeth. Recumbent, or sitting on the load behind, half sunken into the fragrant nest would be Gran'pa and our older cousin, Arnie, brown as a bear, or perhaps our summertime boarders from New York, Mickey and Aaron.

In a rainstorm the porch seemed even more magical, affording an intense sense of shelter, keeping us dry even as sheets of water cascaded off the roof onto the grass. Thunderstorms were another matter since nearly everyone in the family harbored an unreasonable fear of lightning, and before the first detectable rumble ran its course, Mother would shepherd us kids into the house, all windows closed and everyone seated as far away from them as possible. If it happened to be an intense storm we would likely end up in near darkness, sitting on the stairway in the front hall as though at the theater, cringing at each flash visible through the window in the front door below. This might have been fun if it hadn't been for the shrieks from Mother and Aunt Lydia at each bright flash.

I remember being awakened by Dad bursting into my room in the middle of the night and slamming my window shut as, outside, the sky was lighted almost continuously by

*The hayrack was a steel-wheeled wagon, seen here in 1947, designed to carry a carefully built load of loose hay from the field to the barn. Summer visitors from New York, "Mickey" and Aaron Farkas, often helped out, and at one time considered partnering with Dad and buying the farm from Gran'pa.*

*Like any Maine farm building, those at Maple Hill Farm had to withstand the ravages of wind, sun, rain, and snow. In this photo from 1995, we see the house after an uncharacteristic southeast snowstorm.*

the frequent lightning flashes. The light show was accompanied by constant deafening thunder, and the tattoo of the pelting rain and hail sounded almost like a crackling bonfire. That storm was truly frightening and I remember being grateful for the relative shelter of those hall stairs and the uneasy companionship of our entire extended family.

Standing tall among the mature maples and red spruces in the yard on the very top of Maple Hill, the building did at times seem vulnerable to lightning. How effective the yellow-globed lightning rods that stood vigil at intervals along the ridges of both house and barn were in intercepting strikes and grounding them is hard to tell. But in those days they were standard fixtures on most farm buildings. And although nearby trees were occasionally struck with devastating results, to my knowledge the buildings themselves never suffered a strike. During one storm a bolt of lightning at the edge of the pasture across the road struck a maple under which several cows had sought shelter from the downpour. Instantly, a strip of bark was peeled from the trunk from crown to root, and partway down a Guernsey cow intercepted the charge and was killed instantly.

Far more common in my memory are the velvet-like summer evenings passed sitting on the open porch, listening to the singing crickets and the calls of the then-common whip-poor-wills, seasoned with the breeping of the flashing night hawks. Down across the field, along the tree-lined cow path, thousands of fireflies blinked their urgent sensual messages. Being sited on high, well-drained land, and gently swept by almost constant westerly breezes even on otherwise uncomfortable hot summer nights, Maple Hill Farm was practically immune from assaults by mosquitoes and other biting insects, window screens being more of a precaution than a necessity, except to keep out the moths and June bugs.

On a perfect summer evening, after chores, it was not unusual to find, assembled on the porch, my parents, Linda and me, Aunts Lydia and Annie, and one or two of our friends, who delayed as long as possible walking or biking home and thus ending the spell. Sadly, these evenings grew less common once we acquired our first strangely captivating television. Gran'pa might sit with us for a time, but eventually he would get up and repair to his spot on the milkhouse steps, where lost in his own thoughts and memories, he would sit and smoke.

Much later, when in my room I turned off my light to sleep, I would look out my window and see the glowing end of his cigarette each time he took a puff. As my eyes grew accustomed to the gloom, I could make out his motionless figure seated on the top step, hunched forward with elbows resting on his knees.

# CHAPTER THREE

## A DAY IN A BEAUTIFUL NEIGHBORHOOD

As I remember it, the Maple Hill community was a close and friendly one but not in any way intrusive. Nearly everyone was a good neighbor, but for the most part families kept to themselves when it came to things like holidays and social interaction. Our nearest neighbor was down the lane-like road a couple of hundred yards. Old Bessie Longel and her son, John, lived in a farmhouse there, and across the road from them were my Aunt Helen, her husband, Arnold "Dick" Dickinson, and their two boys, our cousins, Arnie and Mike. Mike is younger than me but Arnie is six years older. Because of the family ties, I think it's safe to say the two boys spent a good deal of their childhoods at our place.

Bessie Longel's husband, Avery, I don't remember, but they had exchanged farms with Avery's brother, Frank, and his wife, Marion, before I was born. What prompted this swap I've never known. The farms were adjacent but the farmhouses probably a third of a mile apart. Wind Hover Farm, farther down the hill toward the lake, became the home of Frank and Marion.

Frank and Avery Longel were good, frugal Yankee farmers, and were extremely helpful to my grandfather when he bought Maple Hill Farm with no farming experience. Many times they must have shaken their heads in wonder. The Longel boys kept their dairy herds small, which gave them the opportunity to better manage other elements of family farming, such as raising beef cattle and vegetables, working their woodlots, and even operating a small sawmill. They had tractors long before we did, but for a long time kept two yoke of oxen as well. Dick and Dime were beautiful chestnut-colored Red Durhams, and the other, taller team comprised black-and-white Holsteins whose names escape me. The oxen, stronger and surer-footed—as well as slower—than draft horses were ideally suited for working in the woods.

Avery and Bessie's son, John, a bachelor his whole life, worked around the farm weekends but had a day job at a textile mill in town. Still, he lived at the farm the rest of his life, including the twenty or so years Bessie survived Avery.

*Neighbor Frank Longel (1947) and his wife, Marion (1956), along with his brother Avery and sister-in-law Bessie, were extremely kind and helpful to my grandparents when they first took over Maple Hill Farm.*

The two Longel daughters, Margorie and Elva, lived with their husbands, Henry Davenport and George Tomlinson, in two identical houses the men built with lumber cut on the farm woodlot and sawed out at their sawmill. Henry and George had together run the fish hatchery outside Rangely where George grew up and met the Longel sisters when Henry was transferred to the local hatchery, Townsend Brook, at the foot of Maple Hill. It was a fortunate uniting as far as Linda and I were concerned because the Davenport kids, "Butch" and Marilyn, as well as Joe and Mary Ann Tomlinson, became the core of our childhood gang of friends.

Sadly, this was the tail end of the era of reasonably sized family farms, and Maple Hill, like hundreds of other rural communities around the state, was seeing its farmland and its lovely farmhouses pass from families who had made their livings on the places, to new families with husbands, and increasingly wives, who worked in town.

Soon after the death of Frank Longel, Wind Hover Farm was sold to a non-farming family, as was the Parson place, the next farm down the hill. Bud Lewis, now years retired from his job as an engineer at a mill, still lives in his immaculate farmhouse, but the huge barn was taken down many years ago. The Lewis kids, Henry and Harriet, likewise were active members of our circle, Eddie being a bit young to join in.

*Bessie Longel was a kind and generous neighbor and the grandmother of our buddies, the Davenport and Tomlinson children. We spent countless hours playing around the Longels' scaled-down farm and enjoying Bessie's treats.*

Continuing this trend, farming at the Monroe place up the road had been phased out about the time I was born. It had passed down from Harvey Dillingham, a descendent of the early settlers on the hill, including Isaac Dillingham who reputedly had built the early cape that eventually grew into Maple Hill Farm, and the Johnson farm on the road winding up the hill from North Auburn village was no longer being farmed although years later Al Webster, a livestock dealer, bought the place and used the barn and adjacent field in this capacity.

The only other serious farm on the hill was clear across to the northwest corner, where Lionel and Gladys Hardy ran a dairy operation similar to ours in size but more up to date and efficient. Their older son, Doug, a very capable individual, kept an active interest in the family farm for a few years after high school, which certainly enhanced its operation. The other Hardy children, like the rest of us, soon turned their backs on this hard life with no vacations to pursue other interests.

For most of us kids, growing up on the hill was like being in paradise. The question of security never crossed ours or our parents' minds, and as soon as we were big enough to get around, we did, and were made welcome in just about everybody's household.

My sister Linda's best friend, Marilyn, spent a great deal of time at her grandmother Bessie Longel's place since her parents worked during the day. White-haired Bessie with her wire-rimmed spectacles was still a quintessential Yankee farmer's wife, although a widow and as kindhearted and easy-going as could be. She kept house for her son, "Uncle" John, and served as a loving caretaker for Marilyn.

At about the age of four years, Marilyn began paying visits to Linda at our house. Once she was bundled up and ready to go, Bessie would call up on the phone (we shared an eight-party line) to alert Mother. Then she'd walk her granddaughter out to the road edge and start her on her way. From our second-story kitchen window, Mother would monitor the progress of the little bobbing blonde head until she got close, then Mother went out with Linda to meet her. Later, Mother would call Bessie when Marilyn was ready to return and she would stand watch at the side of the road until her granddaughter had safely returned.

It wasn't long before Linda was returning these visits and soon after was made to drag me along with her. At the Longels' we might be joined by Bessie's other grandkids, Joe and Mary Ann Tomlinson, and under Bessie's relaxed supervision, pretty much given the run of the place.

In true New England fashion you entered Bessie's house by the backdoor, through the "summer kitchen," which in this case was no longer being used as such. It had a day bed, a table, and a few chairs, and was a great place to draw and play games on rainy days. Out back, facing west, there was a glassed-in and somewhat cluttered "piazza" that provided another neat place for unsupervised play. Bessie had no problem with us running up the stairs and taking over the two upstairs bedrooms, including, to the amazement of Linda and me, jumping up and down on the big bed in what Marilyn called the "Humpty-Dumpty room." When we grew tired of roughhousing we'd head downstairs to the kitchen where there might be warm homemade cookies or cupcakes that we washed down with tumblers of fresh milk.

The Longels were among the first families on the hill to invest in a television, which also became an attraction. We crowded on the kitchen day bed to watch *The Howdy Doody Show*, countless corny Westerns, and everyone's favorite first claymation character, Gumby, in fuzzy black and white on a twelve-inch screen. The Longels and Davenports may have been first in our neighborhood to adopt this technology, but within a couple years every house had a set and the quality of the production seemed to match the pace of improved programming.

The absence of rules also applied to play in the Longels' barn, probably because the farm was no longer a serious operation. Without permission, we were allowed to climb around the lofts at will, build tunnels with hay bales, and launch sessions of hide-and-seek to die for. At some point the "big boys"—cousin Arnie, Butch Davenport, and their buddies— all six or seven years older than me, had hung from the peak of the main hay bay a large-diameter rope with a series of knots for seats that served as a swing to fly across the bay when it was empty, starting from various launching areas. Some of those were much higher and scarier than others. We clutched the rope from a perch at one end of the loft and as we jumped we straddled the appropriate knot, wrapping our legs around the tag end below. It was an exhilarating ride even from this modest level, and of course when the older boys were present they showed off by starting their swings from ever farther up on various beams near one end wall. Naturally, they taunted us to follow their daredevil examples, but usually I was too chicken. If memory serves, Joe, Henry, and even Marilyn all risked jumps from higher perches than either Linda or me.

We also had free run of the seldom-used sawmill and the shingle mill, which sat idle in a little thirty-or-more-year-old barn known as the "New Building." We pretended the unguarded saw with its hinged table was a type of guillotine

*That's me in 1951, in one of two prolific cherry trees that grew just outside my Aunt Lydia's hen yard. This lighter-hued variety of fruit was much sweeter and juicier than the dark Bing cherries that grew on another tree in the yard. My mother preserved quarts of these for the delicious pies she baked in the winter.*

and the wooden chute down which the shingles traveled was where the severed heads tumbled into a bushel basket. Of course there was no way we could start the engine that ran this dangerous equipment.

We also were welcome and had great fun, again usually without adult intervention, at the Davenport and Tomlinson homes, as well as at the Lewises and Wellses, and our own farm was also a great place to play, even if the rules were a bit stricter than at the Longels. There were sheds and at times a huge empty barn to play all sorts of games in, and there were fruit trees to climb and raid. My youngish parents were popular with the neighborhood kids because they took an interest in everyone. Mother always served snacks and Dad truly enjoyed kids, paying attention to and teasing them. So attractive was daily life around the place that friends would often elect to stay around, even if it meant they had to help us with our chores.

The new breed of neighbor that was beginning to discover the hill's charms brought with them for us some new perspectives and awareness of other lifestyles. These were often professionals and their families, the wives often graduates of good liberal arts colleges. These families had greater incomes and tastefully decorated their farmhouses without worrying much about the expense. They had shelves stacked with books, and the mothers not only had driver's licenses but their own late-model station wagons. Entire families went skiing during winter vacations and they belonged to the yacht club at Taylor Pond. Some even had cottages and boats at the coast. All of this was quite a revelation to residents of a poor to modestly prosperous farming community like ours.

And they proved to be good neighbors. Their kids played hard right along with us, and we were welcome in their homes and invited to their birthday parties. We were taken to the circus and even plays by these mothers who were also active in the PTA and cultural and public service organizations in town. They bought eggs from Aunt Lydia and were always ready, like the old neighbors, to help whenever asked.

But even though they were accepted and often well-liked there was always a barrier that separated our families from theirs socially. The saddest ramification of this divide, to my eye, was the exclusion of the generous, well-intentioned women from the neighborhood sewing circle—a monthly gathering during the cold-weather months of most of the wives from the hill's older families, where little sewing was accomplished, but much gossip was exchanged.

Our farm provided the first jobs for many of the neighborhood kids, beginning with cousin Arnie. Bearing the double burden of nephew and next-door neighbor, at about the age of twelve Arnie began helping with haying, building the load of loose hay as it was pitched onto the horse-drawn wagon. Reluctantly, he assumed other tasks around the farm, such as hoeing and picking tomatoes, until he was able to escape to a job at Taber's ice cream stand and driving range at the bottom of the hill when he turned sixteen. My friends Joe and Henry likewise began their working careers treading down loose hay along with me, Joe following Arnie's footsteps to Taber's as early as was legal. Henry stayed around most summers, becoming increasingly indispensable right up through high school.

These meager work opportunities also melted a barrier between us and a cluster of families who stayed pretty much to themselves at the far end of the unpaved Beaver Road. The Walker and Mackenzie kids seldom joined us riding bikes, playing scrub baseball, or for birthday parties, but when the opportunity arrived Harold Walker was willing to come work and had his parents' blessing. Harold quickly became a dependable hand and learned more and more jobs, including milking, until he finally joined the Army. He served more than one tour in Vietnam, where he was eventually killed. His brother, Bobby, and then the Mackenzie boys filled in as opportunities developed and helped Dad in all aspects of keeping the farm operating.

Mine is a family of gamblers and Sunday became poker night for Dad, most of my aunts and uncles, visiting relatives, and a few neighbors. The stakes were pennies, and a beer apiece took care of those who didn't drink Pepsi only. Still, the players were serious about their cards. Normally the game began in the downstairs dining room as soon as Dad finished chores. In early summer there still would be lots of daylight and the weekly event provided great fun for us kids as well. We'd start with games like hide-and-seek and red light until it became too dark. Then we'd gather beneath a light bulb in the connecting shed where Arnie would begin terrifying us younger kids with gory, convincingly delivered ghost stories. Eventually we'd end up frightened nearly out of our skins during a game of "ghost" or "mummy," with our older cousin masterfully building that terror as he "hid" in the darkened space while making ever scarier advances on our positions. Then, with a blood-curdling shriek, he'd leap into our midst and grab the first screaming soul he encountered. This normally brought out one or the other of his parents from the card game to yell a warning at him that we all knew would not be followed up on.

# CHAPTER FOUR

## COPING WITH COWS

Our mixed herd of cows made life on the farm not only possible, but frequently very interesting. With around twenty-five milkers at any given time, the total size of the herd, including dry cows (those not producing milk because they were in the later stages of pregnancy), heifers, calves, and a breeding bull was about forty head. Their lives were for the most part satisfying and holistic when compared with some of today's genetically altered, milk-producing machines you see staring vacantly from under a steel roof, wet manure up to their knees and mammoth udders swollen. Large numbered ear tags with coded information are often the only identification these poor beasts ever have. By contrast, we knew our cows by their names, personalities, and quirks.

The herd was about evenly divided between brown-and-white and black-and-white animals. Most of the brown cows were Guernseys, with a few Ashires and Brown Swiss mixed in. These were a bit smaller than the black-and-white Holsteins, and although they produced less milk, theirs was richer, higher in butterfat content, which was one factor that determined the price paid per hundredweight of milk.

Naturally, with this heterogeneous herd, the original breeds became increasingly diluted until there were essentially no purebreds left. Additionally, my father and grandfather were always buying from and selling to old John Stevens, a cattle dealer who lived just above the school in North Auburn village. As a result, our already robustly mixed herd was further diversified by the additions of the odd Jersey or milking Shorthorn. There is little doubt in my mind that the animals bred on our farm benefited through hybrid vigor. Most of the cows were alert, capable, and even intelligent. Most were not polled but rather sported their naturally bestowed horns. This may have led to a relaxed hierarchy in the herd with a little bullying but no real fighting or trouble I can recall.

In 1960 my father legally purchased the farm from my grandfather. Although this didn't change anything domestically, the bulk of the herd became my father's. Up until

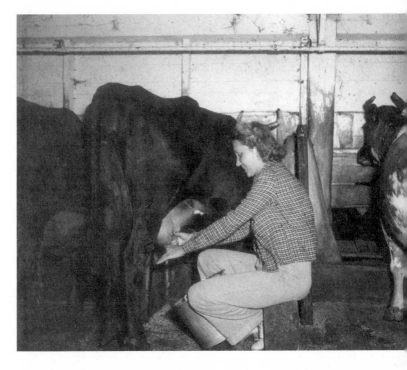

*The milking machine has finished and Mickey "strips" a cow's udder some time in 1947.*

that time about a quarter of the milkers belonged to Dad and we weighed and recorded each pail of milk so the biweekly check from the processor, H. P. Hood, could be divided proportionately. The trend in dairying was already moving toward greater volume and away from maximum fat content, so to increase production a bit Dad purchased a few registered Holsteins that to me seemed like big, dumb creatures, standing taller than any of the veterans, their dorky, hornless heads bobbing. But they adapted to their new home well enough and considerably outproduced their herd mates.

Then followed a little surge in the price for butterfat content. Dad reacted by purchasing a pair of registered Jerseys—small, tawny creatures with lovely faces, big liquid eyes, and long lashes. Their contributions to the milk tank were smaller but rich in cream and flavor and everything that makes fresh milk delicious. There was never a shortage of fresh whole milk in glass half-gallon jugs in our refrigerator. Unpasteurized, unhomogenized, and rich in pale-yellow cream that separated out and floated on top in a thick layer, we drank it by the tall glassful at every meal and as often as we wanted in between.

For many years my father did all the milking because I was too young and Gran'pa never had been very good around cows. At milking time he would fire up the ancient compressor that growled uncertainly from its shelf as it fed compressed air down a galvanized line that ran above the cows hitched in their half stalls. Spigots along the line

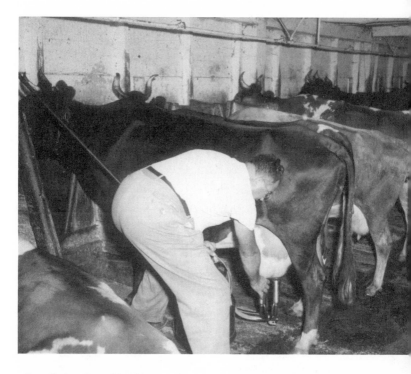

*Aaron Farkas, along with Mickey, one of our summertime boarders from New York, tries his hand at applying the milking-machine cups without losing suction—not as easy as it would appear.*

permitted Dad to connect with rubber hoses the two portable milking units to this source of power. These stainless-steel units consisted of a pail with a tapered throat to collect the milk and a flat lid with a seal that had a small piston on it which clicked back and forth, providing suction to four long rubber-lined cups that were applied to the cows' teats. Two hoses fed the cup unit, one providing the suction, and a second, of clear plastic, allowing you to watch the frothy milk pulse up and into the pail to the rhythm of the clicking piston. If the vacuum was lost at any point, including when the cups were applied, this entire unit lost its grip and fell to the floor. There it would lay sprawled like a four-tentacled octopus, hissing and sucking up sawdust and worse, the disruption causing even the calmest veteran milk cow to dance around and probably step on the thing.

Such an event required that the entire unit be disassembled, any milk in the pail— now contaminated—dumped, and all the hoses, cups, and gaskets washed thoroughly at the milkhouse sink with hot water with a bit of iodine solution.

For too many years Dad was handicapped by this unreliable, erratic equipment that could, without warning, lose compression and cause such disasters in duplicate. At one point his frustration and temper reached the meltdown point and in a rage he actually threw one of the stubborn units out the window and down into the muddy cow yard fifteen feet below.

Eventually, with a new system in service, and with Dad's great experience, the twice-daily milking proceeded calmly and smoothly, the new units pulsing away and being shunted without incident from cow to cow down the long row.

*Gran'pa's old Dodge pickup truck, stripped down and on its way to its final resting place. It was the only truck on the farm until I was ten, and Gran'pa spent many hours simply keeping the thing running.*

During my early youth the milk from the machines was strained and stored in ten-gallon steel milk cans that sat in icy water in a galvanized cooler, not unlike an oversized old-fashioned soda cooler in a country store. Every couple days it would be Gran'pa's job to drive these full cans into town to the Hood plant alongside a railroad siding. He'd first back his old Dodge truck with the wooden-spoked wheels and flat roof up to the milkhouse door. Dad would lift the full cans, dripping water, out of the cooler and roll them on their bottom rims out onto the wooden bed of the ancient vehicle that Gran'pa referred to as his "machine." It wasn't as though Gran'pa was interested in antiques; it was just that this is all we had. A great seat-of-the-pants mechanic, he spent countless hours fiddling with it, even making parts to keep it running—time, no doubt, that could have been better spent on any number of tasks around the farm.

Still, when we were young, neither Linda nor I would pass up a chance to putter into town with Gran'pa. We knew that after the cans had been unloaded, emptied, and rinsed, the recessed lids replaced with a couple ringing smites from a hammer, and the empties reloaded into the truck bed, that he would probably bring us out a chocolate milk. And this was no ordinary chocolate milk. It came in little half-pint bottles made of thick glass with a rough pebbly finish like real milk bottles, water droplets condensing on the outside because of the ice-cold contents—the smoothest, creamiest chocolate milk on the planet. I have yet to taste its equal.

By the time I was too old and "cool" to risk embarrassment riding in the dilapidated truck with my rough-looking, stubbly-chinned grandfather (even for the world's best chocolate milk), H. P. Hood had all its producers switched over to stainless-steel bulk tanks that kept an even temperature, and kept the milk and cream from separating by means of a big paddle that rotated constantly. Every other morning around 4 a.m. a gleaming tank truck would come by to collect the milk. The driver tabulated the volume and left a slip in accordance with which the milk checks would later be cut.

I remember being awakened by the arrival of the truck in the midst of a "Nor' easter" blizzard, the air brakes hissing, headlights and backup lights exaggerating the fury of the wildly swirling snow. Despite all this the unperturbed driver was completing his appointed rounds, backing the heavy truck through the accumulating drifts as deftly as if they weren't even there.

Beginning around the middle of May, when our well-drained pasture had thoroughly dried and the new green grass had been given a start, until mid-October, our milk cows had the privilege of being let outdoors for the day after the morning milking—there to fill their bellies with fresh green grass, exercise, and take their ease in the shade on hot summer days, chewing their collective cuds and hopefully concentrating on producing milk. In late afternoon they were called in to get their high-protein grain mix before the evening chores. Normally, just a few repetitions of "Come Boss, Come Boss" by my father standing at a window overlooking the pasture was enough to get the first small groups of cows and then the entire herd materializing from the various corners and heading toward the barn. This handiest of several pastures consisted of eight acres of open fields that were formerly an apple orchard, and an equal amount of cutover woods. Over the summer the woods became laced with trails winding beneath the trees and through the thickets of alder, blackberries, and ground junipers we knew as "ground hemlocks." Sometimes a stubborn cow or two chose to ignore Dad's invitation or somehow didn't hear it. It would then be my job to search them out and encourage them on their way.

At the barn the cows ascended the sloping rock ramp leading up to the eastern end of the tie-up or milking bay, or simply the "cow barn." Once inside they wasted little time locating an empty stall, where as fast as he could manage, Dad would hitch them with loose-fitting chain collars. When most of the herd was inside and the rest climbing the ramp I'd help hitch them, being careful of any dangerously bobbing horned head as I reached to get a chain that had slid down the smooth round post that was part of the stanchion.

Next, out in the scaffolded center bay, or hay barn, Dad would trundle bags of grain along a row of long hinged trapdoors that could be let down to reveal the cows expectant faces. He'd measure out each cow's apportioned ration with a much dented graniteware bowl while I cleaned out the stalls of the poor calves, who were not allowed out with their milk-producing mothers for obvious reasons. We'd then go into the house to eat an early supper and then it was back through the connecting shed to the barn for evening chores. While Dad began the milking I'd mix a malty-smelling formula for the younger calves and feed and water the older ones. If Buck and Don the draft horses were in their box stalls under the mow across the hay barn, I'd lug them water from the cow barn in the five-gallon buckets the calf formula had come in. I learned early how to swing the buckets up to rest on the ledge of their square openings without slopping out too much water, and to tilt them so the gentle boys could slake their mammoth thirsts.

Then, for a time, I'd stay around to carry the pails of milk into the milkhouse, dumping them into the filter-lined strainers that fed the tank then releasing the cows that had been milked for their night in the pasture. These were enjoyable times to spend with my father and we talked and joked about the day's events, or better yet he'd tell stories of his own growing up. Still, with the long summer evenings, I was grateful to be excused early to run down the road and join the kids heard playing outside.

By late summer the pasture adjacent to the barn would be grazed down to the point where it could no longer satisfy the herd, and since the haying had been completed in the forty-acre field across the road, this became the new daytime pasture. This meant the cows needed to be shepherded twice each day across the lightly traveled road that ran past our farm.

In late afternoons it was my chore to monitor the crossing, prevent renegades from darting into our main driveway and bee-lining into the hay barn in search of any open sack of grain, as well as to round up the stragglers in this much larger area. This wasn't that difficult a job but it was one I dreaded above all others because I hated delaying the car or two that might be inconvenienced by the unhurried procession. I felt like melting into the tarmac each time a crossing cow lifted her tail and let go, splattering the road with a runny trail of sticky green manure, that the driver would then be forced to cross. I don't believe there was any law requiring us to scrape such unpleasant obstacles off the roadway, and it never occurred to us to initiate such a courtesy.

Even greater was my unfounded fear that perhaps one of my friends or classmates from school would happen by, catching me in my shabby workclothes at what I deemed the demeaning task of guiding the cows toward our embarrassingly weather-beaten farm buildings. Such were the anxieties and vanities of my youth.

From time to time a cow heavy with calf would be brought in from a separate pasture it had been sharing with our freshening heifers and kept with the milking herd so Dad could check it for signs of imminent calving.

He knew the signs very well and seldom misjudged exactly which day to confine the mother-to-be to prevent her from bearing and then hiding her newborn in the wooded pasture. But occasionally Dad would be fooled, and it is amazing how well a woods-wise cow can hide her calf when she suspects separation will occur once the calf is found. In a wooded pasture like ours with underbrush, boulders, and spreading, prickly ground junipers, finding a motionless calf instinctively curled up like a fawn is no easy matter. The mother is of no help, staying clear of her baby except to let it suckle a couple times a day so as not to betray its location. I spent many hours, sometimes half a day, trying to locate these well-hidden treasures. Often, when I got lucky and unknowingly very close, the cow would finally betray the exact spot by suddenly bawling and marching purposefully toward me in a protective and even threatening manner.

Once the wobbly legged calf, already licked clean, was discovered there was little choice but to hoist the sweet-smelling little bundle across my shoulders, holding its legs, and start for the barn. The concerned cow would invariably follow, bawling her displeasure and occasionally coming close to sniff or even lick her confiscated youngster. I was late even for my senior prom date because of difficulty in locating just such a well-hidden, woods-born calf.

We kept our yearling heifers in their own section of pasture below the hayfield. Across the road a cow path with trees on both sides ran down between two stone walls, forming a truly sylvan lane, the years-old ruts worn deeply between increasingly exposed rocks and boulders, and the path bathed in the dappled sunlight that filtered down through the rustling leaves. This arrangement caused us additional frustration at times because the heifers were agile and bold if not actually diabolical, and could find ways through the rickety barbed-wire fence that snaked through the woodlot below and defined their eastern boundary. Usually they wouldn't wander far, and they possessed homing instincts that more often than not enabled them to return to their legal range on their own. There were surely times we were never even aware they'd left. Other times a call from a neighbor alerted us that another challenging heifer chase was in order.

A worst-case situation unfolded one rainy Sunday afternoon in late summer. Normally we tried to limit work on Sundays to chores, or perhaps picking a box or two of tomatoes for a good customer. But when bad weather

plagued the early haying season, we had to take advantage of
good haymaking days, Sundays included. That day the steady
rain outside saved us from this fate and typically on such days
we'd be gathered in the living room, Dad snoozing in his easy
chair, Mother reading, and me sprawled on the floor with the
dogs, drawing. Linda would likely be in her room listening to
her stack of 45-rpm records and leafing through movie
magazines. On the day in question, the jangling telephone
rudely interrupted our domestic tranquility. It was Mr. Fuller,
who operated a garage and welding shop clear down on the
Turner Road. Obviously agitated, he informed us that he had
just chased our young stock out of his garden.

I sat in the backseat sulking as Mother drove us down
the hill, around the lake shore, and a mile or so up Route 4
to Fuller's place, where Dad and I stepped out into his yard.
It was raining hard and the temperature was about fifty-five
degrees. Our sweatshirts and jeans began soaking up the
cold water like a sponge as Fuller angrily pointed out the
offenders huddled beneath some trees beyond his precious
garden. I'd have liked to have shot them.

Once they spotted us heading toward them the critters
lit out for home, trotting ahead though the sodden underbrush
and stopping periodically to watch us floundering behind.
We kept on their tails, fording Townsend Brook, which was
running up to our knees and presented a muddy,

hummocky bank on either side. We were slapped by saturated bushes that unloaded their reservoirs upon us, and we stumbled as we traveled the uneven ground, tripping on the late-summer vines and runners that seemed to wrap themselves around our legs.

Unerringly, the heifers led us through the less-familiar lowland woods, then up the hillside into our own woodlot and on to the pasture fence, returning as always precisely to the breech in the old fence that this time had been caused by a fallen tree limb.

I shivered with the cold, waiting impatiently for Dad to finish a temporary repair of the fence. By then the rain had stopped. Soaked through, we continued on toward home and chores, now impervious to the wetness. From every leaf and needle the sparkling droplets glistened like prisms catching the late-afternoon sun that found its way into an opening among the now-torn clouds. Not for the first time, Dad pointed out to me the spot where he had encountered and missed a giant whitetail buck, and somehow our shanghaied day of leisure seemed like an inconsequential loss when compared to our rain-drenched adventure.

# CHAPTER FIVE

## A BIT OF LEARNING

Perched on a little rise across the road from the lake at the edge of North Auburn village, the Charles P. Wight School showcased all that was considered modern, efficient, and starkly handsome in 1950. That is to say it was a white-clapboarded rectangular box divided on the inside by a spacious T-shaped hall/cafeteria into four classrooms, a small teachers' room/office, boys' and girls' bathrooms, and a kitchen no larger than ours at home. The classrooms were bright and high-ceilinged with a full row of large windows along one wall. It served between ninety and a hundred students from the rural communities of West Auburn, North Auburn, Maple Hill, Hersey Hill, Skillings Corner, as well as a handful of kids from the far-flung reaches of Minot and Turner who lived too far off the school-bus routes of those neighboring towns.

Charles P. Wight School replaced the one-room school attended by my father and his siblings, as well as a similar establishment in West Auburn. Linda was a member of the first kindergarten to initiate the brand-new building; the building had not been completed at the start of school in September, and the classes were held at the North Auburn Grange Hall. When the project was completed later in the fall, the pupils packed up their books and pencil boxes and walked together through the village to inaugurate the sparkling facility.

Mrs. Skillings, a robust, imposing woman, served as principal and could be a convincing disciplinarian when called upon, but was generally fair-minded. She also taught the kindergarten, introducing the new conscripts to the patterns of education at C. P. Wight, as well as the behavior that would be expected of them. From Mrs. Skillings, those who didn't already know them learned the basic colors, the alphabet, numbers, and printing their names, this latter on yellow, lightly lined paper with every other widely spaced line broken so there would be no mistaking the relationship between upper and lower case letters. Across the hall, Miss Farmer and, later, Mrs. Brookings taught the first and second graders, and at the school's other end,

*Go Rinny! When Rin Tin Tin from the 1950s television show, along with a couple of the cast members, had a stopover at the Auburn airport in 1957, George Tomlinson, the facility manager, alerted the neighbors. Here with Rin Tin Tin, from the left, are Mary Ann and Joe Tomlinson, Kathy Wells, Henry Lewis, Linda, Eddie Lewis, and me.*

Mrs. Hammond, third and fourth. Across from her, Mrs. Bibber prepared the fifth and sixth graders for the big step up to Webster Junior High School in town.

Students and teacher had two years to get to know each other's weaknesses and strengths. If one year you found yourself a rookie, a bit intimidated by the more advanced class sharing the room with you, the next you'd be one of the big dogs, showing off your confidence to the new crop of underclassmates. By this system I caught up room-wise to my pal, Joe Tomlinson, a year older than me, three different times before he left C. P. Wight for keeps, climbing onto the big yellow bus that transported the older kids to a wider, less-coddled experience in town.

Unless it was raining we got to play outside during a fifteen-minute recess at 10 each morning, as well as for whatever time was left of the noon hour break after eating lunch. Hot lunch cost a quarter and was eaten in the cafeteria; cold lunch was eaten with one or two fellow tin-pailers in one's own room. The hot lunches were prepared by Mrs. Wilson and a helper. Because of the small numbers, and Mrs. Wilson's industry, her meals, although from the same district-wide menu with basically the same ingredients, were much better than what we'd get later at junior high.

There was no fooling around during lunch and even talking loudly was discouraged. A clean-plate policy was in effect and you were expected to eat *everything* on your tray. Fortunately, the cook got to know which dishes were next-to-impossible for a particular pupil to swallow, and she'd then dish out a very small portion. But you were never allowed to skip anything entirely unless you were smart enough to have brought your lunchbox. For me, it was the baked beans—I just couldn't get them down, although they had actually been baked in the oven and lots of my peers said they were delicious.

The tables were dismissed one at a time as soon as everyone at it was finished and sitting quietly with hands folded. Seating was not assigned, but of course cliques monopolized favored tables. Peer discipline came into play if you got stuck with some clown at your table whose high jinks kept you from being dismissed, returning the empty tray, and getting your "wraps," the term used by this aging faculty for your coat and other outside clothing.

The lucky kids who lived in North Auburn village got to walk home for lunch. We'd sometimes get them to pick us up nickel candy at Lou Libby's store on their way back to school.

The grounds at C. P. Wight were expansive as at many rural schools, and after lunch were filled with activity and the happy sounds of children enjoying themselves. Beside two sets of swings with attached slides, one set much larger than the other, there were seesaws and a merry-go-round for the younger pupils. The myth persisted that by pumping amazingly hard, Erland Holbrook had succeeded in making a full swing around the steel tube from which the swings were suspended, wrapping the chains around behind him.

There were two fields suitable for baseball, one of them also good for strictly touch football. Both were used extensively during the appropriate seasons. The girls took out soft, smooth soccer-sized balls for dodge ball. Tag was also popular, and sometimes escalating contests of red rover that were usually stopped by the teacher on duty before someone got hurt. Some winters the ball field was flooded for skating. Since I didn't own a pair of skates that fit and it took me forever to get them on and tied, I usually passed on this popular activity, hoping for snow so the damn rink would be buried and we could get everybody building snow forts. During the fifth and sixth grades, due largely to the influence of a new, mature-thinking friend who had moved to Maple Hill from Philips, I spent as much time playing dodge ball, because the girls were involved, as I did playing baseball.

Behind the school, a series of below-grade basement windows were protected by recessed wells lined with half sections of galvanized culvert set on end, with a natural floor of crushed rock covered by fallen leaves and twigs. These little pockets became receptacles for the occasional garter snake as well as handsome spotted salamanders and adorable little efts like orange-red jewels with limbs so tiny they appeared translucent. By kneeling you could just about reach the bottom, and we'd dig around, risking the spiders we knew were in there, to find them. Salamanders are fascinating creatures to hold and watch but we were not allowed to keep them. Whenever a well-meaning teacher caught us admiring one she made us return it to what I now realize was essentially the prison it had fallen into and from which it could not hope to escape.

*Linda and me with the family's recently purchased Plymouth in 1950.*

*Despite small differences, like rural kids everywhere, my sister Linda and I, seen here in 1951, depended a lot on each other for companionship and support. Three years difference in ages didn't amount to much as we grew older.*

There was a dark side even to our naïve, sheltered little school community. The inexplicable mean streak that plagues children everywhere reared its ugly head at Charles P. Wight where there was no justification for it whatsoever. This manifested itself in the senseless verbal abuse and taunting endured by a few unlucky individuals who had been singled out because they were very poor or may have been a bit slow finishing their work, but mostly couldn't defend themselves. These kids became the lepers of our school and when out of hearing of the nearest teacher, they were subject to insults and ridicule, although they were seldom if ever assaulted physically. Following Linda's example I never participated in this inexcusable behavior, and as I grew older would suggest to the tormentors they knock it off. But, regrettably, I never pressed my natural advantage as the tallest and, as a result of the farm work, one of the strongest boys in the school, to really come down hard on the tormentors.

In Mrs. Bibber's fifth and sixth grades, after saluting the flag and reciting the Lord's Prayer, you began each day's work by doing a math drill from examples written on the blackboard by one of the teacher's pets. Order was important to Mrs. Bibber and your sheet of math paper first needed to be exactly divided into the proper number of spaces, each labeled. Next, you solved your sums, remainders, products, and quotients, worked out the fraction and decimal problems, and even converted Roman numerals. If you got an answer wrong, you worked on it until you got it right— and until your drill paper was perfect, including commas between the hundredth and thousandth places, you wouldn't be going out at recess.

Also on the blackboard on Mondays there would be written a short poem or stanzas from longer works of poetry that had to be committed to memory and written out perfectly, by heart, at week's end. This also included punctuation. In retrospect, this seems a numbing exercise that would breed hatred for verse, but for me at least it was not unpleasant and provided an introduction to many popular poets and poems. I can still recite a few beginning lines from Masefield's "Sea Fever," Longfellow's "Evangeline" and "The Children's Hour," and bits of poems by Joyce Kilmer, Alfred Noyes, and others—not from my literature classes much later in college, but rather from Mrs. Bibber's relentless insistence upon familiarization by rote.

Only then came the daily lessons in math, science, and English grammar, split into two sessions of each because of the two grade levels in the room. Whenever Mrs. Bibber moved on to the other class you had the chance to do your assignments and, as a result, seldom had homework.

If you finished your assignments early, you were expected to read one of the books from the little library at the back of the room if you hadn't brought your own. With prior permission you could work at the counter, also in the back, designing and creating dioramas in the big cubicles that had been built along one wall for storage but which were often never used. Not everyone jumped at this opportunity, but I loved it, drawing and coloring the three background panels and taping them in. Next, if you were creative, you made clay creatures and figures and constructed objects like fences and buildings from other materials. If you lacked imagination, or simply were not inspired, you could cop out and dress out the scene with plastic toys. My favorite themes were logging and wildlife, having gotten over an obsession with dinosaurs.

Mrs. Bibber valued creativity and loved music, and each Friday afternoon after lunch the entire student body was assembled around the piano in the cafeteria. While she played we sang old American standbys, patriotic songs, silly songs, and the more innocent popular tunes such as "The Red Red Robin." This was all fine until somewhere around the fourth grade I got it into my head that it really wasn't cool to be sitting there singing these corny tunes, and I simply refused to join in. Luckily, my disciplinary record was otherwise spotless and my mute presence was tolerated rather than punished. And when I went through a stage of writing poems—most of them terrible, even for a fifth grader—Mrs. Bibber was characteristically supportive and invited me to read them aloud to my patient classmates, even setting one entitled "New England States" to music.

A few times each school year the relative peace in the class-room was jarringly disrupted by the incessant ringing of all the school's electric bells. The first thought was always a fire drill, which most of us welcomed because fire drills inter-rupted class work, got you outside, and ate up time. But this cacophony continued unabated long enough to signify only one thing: the dreaded air raid drill. *No one* enjoyed these. This was of course during the Cold War, and civil prepared-ness was the only means our government could think of to perhaps save some lives when the inevitable nuclear attack was launched by the Soviet Union. Each county and some towns had their Civil Defense coordinators, roughly parallel to today's Homeland Security personnel. I wasn't sure how much everyone else at school worried about this impending Armageddon, but I worried about it plenty, and if you watched the news at all it was difficult not to.

As the bells continued, Mrs. Bibber lined us all up exactly as for a fire drill or recess. Being the most experi-enced students, we got to go last, following Mrs. Hammond's third and fourth graders down the hall, then down the steep wooden stairs into the capacious, high-ceilinged concrete basement with it mammoth furnace and network of plumbing. There, we filled in the final opening on the floor space, sinking to our knees on the hard floor (kept spotless by custodian and bus driver Howard

Thomas), putting our heads down with our hands clasped behind our necks. The lights would be turned off except for a couple eerie emergency lights, and we'd keep this position long enough to imagine how terrible the real thing would be, wondering how badly the blast would hurt, or, worse, what it would be like to be incinerated. I had little faith that this basement could withstand a blast from an atom bomb, and knew where I'd want to be in the case of an actual attack: with my parents.

Eventually some wise guy would emit a suppressed giggle that led Mrs. Skillings to yank him up and off the floor by his shirt and half march, half drag the offender up the stairs and into her office. When the lights were switched back on, one of the teachers would point out a grim-looking stockpile of drinking water in olive-drab cans and cartons of rations that were supposed to get us through the first week or two until the worst of the radiation passed. "And then what?" you couldn't help wondering.

Thus informed and sobered, we, the first generation of the Atomic Age, marched in an orderly fashion back to our classrooms to resume the important work of our enlightenment.

# CHAPTER SIX

## ALL CREATURES

The rustling in the wall beside my bed was definitely a notch or two louder than that made by the typical mouse or even squirrel; and since its source appeared to respond to my rapping and my voice I was reasonably sure I had discovered the whereabouts of my missing pet groundhog, Yogi. A trip up the stairs into the attic revealed the story. Yogi, who pretty much had the run of the house, must have been exploring the unused attic rooms and fallen into one of the open spaces between studs that led down to our second floor apartment. Being a bit fat, Yogi was wedged tightly between the lathes that sheathed the rough studs on either side, and although we didn't yet know it, he was stuck head downward, his belly facing my room, his back toward the living room.

Although I'm certain Dad had a hundred more important things to do, in short order he had my bed moved away from the wall and was trying to gauge where to start boring in with an auger. Yogi's whimpering became fainter and justifiably we feared that he was running short on air. A second check with a flashlight from above revealed Yogi's inverted position, and father's entry hole was perfectly placed just below his snout. As Dad sawed and pulled away sections of lathe Yogi revived enough to lend a hand, employing his effective rodent incisors to gnaw away at the restraining strips. Within a few minutes we were easing from the opening the plaster dust–coated body of one very happy groundhog who expressed his relief with unmistakable squeals and whimpers of joy.

We were as relieved as Yogi was, and as Mother swept up the mess, he rehydrated himself with water and milk, and filled his empty belly with apple wedges, vanilla wafers, and Rice Krispies.

Yogi had been a member of the household for over a year by then, and from the beginning of his stay, when he was a bright-eyed juvenile the size of a gerbil, he displayed a strong personality, a pleasing, playful nature, and a healthy (usually) curiosity. He appeared to enjoy his nearly four-year association with us, which didn't justify the fact I had stolen him from his mother one fine Memorial Day afternoon.

Dad was cruising a woodlot in nearby Wales and I was along for the fun of it. As we were bumping down a one-lane gravel road in the old station wagon, a groundhog ran across the track ahead of us with the noticeable baggage held by her teeth, kitten-fashion. Never one to miss a close-up look at any species of wildlife, I was out the door and in hot pursuit seconds after Father hit the brakes. Mother chuck ran up a grassy bank to her den and dove inside, leaving her helpless kit on the dirt stoop. I picked up and carried the youngster back to the car and had little trouble talking Dad into letting me keep it.

Although only ten, I knew as well as Dad that the little guy belonged with his mother. Of course woodchucks, as groundhogs are usually called in Maine, were and still are plentiful and considered pests by many farmers, most of whom are delighted when someone offers to use them as targets. Still, Yogi was the only wild creature we ever kept as a pet that was not brought to us by a confused cat or by someone who inadvertently had disturbed a nest of babies while working in the woods or around the farm.

From the start, Yogi took to life in our home with relish. He was just old enough to eat all manner of greens and fruit without coaxing. But we soon recognized his preference for Rice Krispies in milk, which became his staple, along with vanilla wafer cookies. These he ate by the dozen, sitting

93

*Yogi the groundhog, or woodchuck, as they are called in Maine, was an interesting pet who spent a couple years with us inside the house and another year and a half either hibernating or living in a burrow alongside the barn. Here he is in 1961, eating an apple after waiting for me to safely walk him down to the nearby trees so he could select a drop.*

upright and turning them in his dexterous black paws. He was very playful and whenever I ruffled his sloping forehead, he would arch his back, tail bottle-brushed, and regard me sideways while emitting a stuttering throaty growl. He'd wrestle my hand vigorously but seldom bit down hard enough to cause more than a minor pinch.

Yogi spent the first six months in a large cage that took up the entire width of one end of my small room. There was a cozy hay-lined cabin at one end, and a large wire-meshed exercise pen at the other that contained the sawdust-filled litter box he used scrupulously, as well as his feeding area. We let Yogi out of his cage each evening when we gathered in the living room to watch TV, and during the day whenever I wanted to play with him. But that wasn't enough to suit Yogi, who began noisily pulling at the mesh with his teeth, until we finally let him have the run of the house, leaving the door at the top open so he could use his litter box, sleep in his den, and eat from his tray of fresh selections. He seldom got into trouble, but one time he stripped the insulation off the electrical cord to the clothes dryer without getting electrocuted. Yogi was in the habit of greeting visitors at the door, and when the serviceman arrived to repair the cord he waddled out to investigate.

"Well I'll be darned," the man said from his hands and knees, practically looking Yogi in the eye. "You really do have a woodchuck!" Then, looking apologetically up at Mother he confessed, "You know, when you told us that on the phone we figured you were just covering up the fact you had rats."

After a couple years Yogi got restless during the summer weather. We left open for him a hall window and since we lived upstairs he'd climb out onto the porch roof to bask in the sunshine and get fresh air. He took to jumping off the edge into a huge lilac bush, which broke his fall, and from beneath the porch would range out onto the lawn and into the garden for fresh treats. We always caught him and lugged him back inside. Our two dogs, Sandy and Rocky, would ignore Yogi in the house, but my parents figured it might be a different story out of doors. Besides, in those easygoing times, it was not unusual for neighbors' dogs to pass through, and we were sure they represented a threat. Eventually we made the decision to release Yogi a mile or so away in a grown-over pasture off a gravel road that had an ideal mix of thick underbrush and grassy openings, with no ranging farm dogs nearby.

He started exploring his new home with great interest as soon as we let him out of the car, ignoring us entirely as we nervously watched his perambulations. It was not without both apprehension and sorrow that we got back into the car without our furry friend and slowly drove away.

## Respite

*Drawing the mowing machine was hard work for the horses on a hot day, and mowing was demanding on the driver, as well. Here, Dad rests Buck and Don in the shade and takes a well-earned breather himself.*

## Milk Cans

*Until the milk processor switched over to bulk tanks and tank trucks, farmers brought in their cooled milk in stainless steel milk cans each day. Here, Dad rolls the cans onto the bed of Gran'pa's old pickup, while Gran'pa waits and our trusty farm dogs, Rocky and Sandy, look on.*

## August

*After milk, tomatoes were our most important product. Each year Dad and Gran'pa set in around 3,000 plants by hand. These provided lots of weeding and hoeing opportunities for everyone. Unstaked and dependent upon rainwater entirely, each plant produced about a bushel of fruit.*

## Last Crop

*We seldom raised potatoes for market, but always put in a couple rows for family use. They were the last crop harvested, after the tops had died and shriveled. On a cheerless day in late October, Gran'pa digs up the hills, exposing the knobby tubers.*

## Tossing Pulpwood

*Woods work was done in the winter, when there was no fieldwork to be done and the ground was frozen. Here, Dad tosses pulpwood onto a pile behind the barn, just as mud season and the end of such activity sets in.*

## Twitching Out

*Saw logs were sometimes cut in the woodlot and sold for cash, or taken to a sawmill. Rather than taking them across the fields to the road with the horses, Dad dragged or twitched the logs individually to a brow where they could be picked up with a truck.*

## The Scoot

*The horse-drawn scoot built by Gran'pa could be used to carry pulpwood piled across the carriage, or saw logs piled parallel to the carriage. We kids enjoyed riding on it as the horses pulled it along the well-worn trails, causing the scoot to flex and rock. Here, Dad takes the scoot across an early-spring rill, heralding the end of the season.*

## Approaching Storm

*Nothing ruins good hay so much as rain, which also can make it dangerous to put in the barn because of spontaneous combustion. Like all farmers, Dad tried to plan haying according to the forecast, but these were seldom perfect, and invariably some hay got rained on in the fields each year. Here, an August thundershower threatens to break before the load reaches the safety of the barn.*

## Building the Load

*The steel-wheeled hayrack was designed for building a solid load of interlocking loose hay as it was pitched on from the field. Here, I intercept a final forkful of hay that will be tramped down into place before heading to the barn..*

## Turkeys in the Spruce Trees

*One November afternoon we returned from town to find the entire flock of domestic white turkeys roosting in the two tall red spruces along the driveway. Some had made it clear to the tops by hopping and flapping up one limb at a time. Before evening, they voluntarily descended the trees in the same manner.*

## Rite of Spring

*After a long winter confined to their stalls, the cows were ready to enjoy the pasture, with its luxurious fresh grass, once the fields had dried out. Most cows went out eagerly but with characteristic reserve, while others gamboled out into the pasture like young deer.*

## Hidden Treasure

*Usually, pregnant cows about to deliver were confined to the barn for the event. Occasionally, Dad was fooled by the signs and a calf was born outside in the pasture, often well hidden by its mother in the lower wooded section. Here, Rocky and I come upon a cow with its new calf not as well hidden as most.*

## Saw Rig

*This formidable-looking rig made short work of cutting stove-length firewood from longer sections of hardwood. The operator tilted the table, with the wood positioned on it, into the snarling blade. Here, I collect chunks that had been allowed to fall off the end. Other times, I held onto the short ends as Dad ran the wood through, and then tossed the severed ends into the truck or woodshed.*

## Applejack

*Years later, when Dad had switched over to raising beef cattle, Linda and her husband, Les, presented him with Applejack the donkey as the herd mascot. He took his work seriously and once broke the leg of a visiting bull with a well-placed kick. The bull had to be destroyed and Dad had to compensate the owner. With Applejack are Mrs. Mooley and her calf. She was the last resident cow on the farm.*

*Maple Hill Farm as it appears today.* Barbara Trafton

*An aerial view of the farm in the mid-1960s.*

Six weeks later, around the end of September, my grandfather came up the back stairs and announced, "That woodchuck of Getty's, I t'ink he come back."

It was with pure delight that I flew down the stairs to find a leaner, more fit Yogi in the big hay-barn doorway, arching his back and delivering his playful growl. He allowed me to pick him up, and was happy to come inside for some of his favorite treats, but made it clear he did not again intend to become an indoor groundhog.

Yogi dug a burrow next to the north end of the ell next to the tomato and vegetable gardens. He gratefully accepted handouts, but lived largely independently until it was time for him to hibernate in late October—something he hadn't done while living indoors.

He emerged from his den in late March about one-third the size he'd been the previous fall. I left him food daily until the new green shoots burst forth in May, and he again became self-reliant. He relocated to the south side of the barn, digging his den alongside an unused rock ramp that led to a door a dozen feet above the ground level. He had learned about dogs and stayed close to his den unless Dad or I happened to be around.

In September Yogi would wait until I got home from school so I could accompany him the hundred feet or so to the bases of the closest apple trees, where under my protection he could select a juicy drop, usually a Wealthy, and lug it back to the rock pile for consumption. If one of the mellow draft horses came by and tried to take the apple from him, Yogi would simply turn his back to it and continue eating. Sadly, Yogi had not dug his den deep enough, possibly because of the rock base that extended below ground, and although he began hibernation in his sleekest shape ever, he failed to emerge from his winter quarters come spring.

Maple Hill Farm had always been home to a variety of creatures besides the income-producing dairy cows and Buck and Don, the durable team of draft horses that powered the operation. Like every rural farm in the fifties we always had a dog or two to act as watchdogs as well as companions. If a dog caught on to chasing cattle, especially young stock in the right direction, that was a bonus, but it was nothing we had the time or ability to bring about by actual training. A dark mixed-breed named Buddy was my father's all-time favorite. But Buddy died before I was old enough to remember him. Dad told many stories, or at least a few, frequently repeated, about Buddy's skill at surprising raccoons that were raiding the corn and quickly treeing them at the edge of the woods for my father to shoot.

*Linda in 1947, the year before I was born, with the legendary Buddy. According to Dad's stories, Buddy could herd cows, tree marauding raccoons, guard the farm, take care of us children, and if given a chance probably fly an airplane.*

They would be skinned, their pelts stretched and dried, and during the forties especially, resulted in a little cash along with the riddance of a garden pest. Buddy was also good at rounding up milk cows at chore time, and with little direction would chase escaped heifers back into their pasture.

Sandy, supposedly a collie-shepherd mix, was the first dog I remember. He did look a lot like a German shepherd but was much smaller than this mix would lead one to expect, probably weighing not much over thirty pounds. Sandy was a gentle dog with good manners and had no interest in chasing either raccoons or cows. He was good at ferreting out the nests of meadow voles while we were making loads of loose hay and would then devour the squirming pink contents. Sandy was served Pard brand canned dog food along with scraps in the evening and he slept in the house. He lived to fourteen or so and during his final year of life had to be carried outside a few times a day, so he could drag his failing hindquarters around the yard and do his business.

Although supposedly the same mix, Rocky was a different story altogether. He was a powerful dog with a thick red coat not unlike a golden retriever, and weighed about sixty pounds. He was an excellent watchdog, loved his family, and with a lot of coaxing would chase the cows with me once I got them moving. But Rocky was largely indifferent to herding and seldom participated without encouragement. He had several bad habits that cost him plenty of trouble and discomfort and eventually led to his early demise. One was chasing cars. Not all of them, but he'd select the odd vehicle from time to time and run alongside it for seventy yards, barking and biting at the tires. Neither admonition nor swats across the snout would deter him from this dangerous sport for long. Once when he misjudged his clearance he was pulled beneath a panel truck, and rolled yelping out behind. Remarkably there were few noticeable effects, other than a day or two of stiffness and an aversion to the practice for a few weeks.

Like most farm dogs, Rocky had not been neutered and possessed a raging libido. A bitch in season anywhere within a couple miles would draw him like a moth to a porch light. He'd stay away as long as the action warranted, and then would drag home, sometimes as long as a week or more later. He would be leaner and suffering varying states of disfigurement from battles with rivals unknown to us. There were times his snout and forehead appeared to be covered by at least as much scar tissue as hair. Once he made it back home, Dad would clean the bites, put a salve such as Rawleigh's ointment on the worst of them, and Rocky would do little but rest and eat for a few days before returning to his normal routines. A litter of feral dogs looking much like him was attributed to Rocky, and was hunted down by the warden for chasing and killing deer. Rocky brought the sole surviving pup to the farm and Aunt Annie made considerable progress taming the handsome youngster, but before the transition was completed he was hit by a car and killed.

Rocky met his own fate similarly down on busy Route 4

that ran north–south alongside the eastern base of the hill a mile and a half from the farm, where he was hit by a car and killed while on one of his adventures. His carcass was spotted by a carpenter who was doing work at the farm for my parents. Rocky must have been about ten years old at the time.

This casual approach to keeping a dog, neglecting such important practices as licensing, neutering, and keeping dogs at home, was not exclusive to my parents back then, but attitudes were beginning to change for the better. We loved our dogs and they were important members of the family.

*Trouble the beagle, my father's "rabbit-hunting dog," and Heather, our first pedigreed Old English sheepdog puppy. Trouble became a fine pet but never amounted to much of a hunter. Heather became not only a wonderful pet, but the mother of several large litters of beautiful puppies.*

By the time Trouble the beagle came to live with us, responsible pet care played a greater part in the picture. Still, even though she had her tags and shots, Trouble managed, before being spayed, one escapade with a local bluetick hound that resulted in a litter of cute hound-mix puppies, all but one of which was placed in a good home. We kept a male, Harry Hound, who wandered a bit, but mostly only around the fields close by and became a lethal stalker of woodchucks, which are not easily beaten to their dens. I was in high school by this time and was still

*In the mid-sixties my mother decided she would try her hand at raising Old English sheepdogs, a rare dog breed in Maine at the time. For seven or eight years it was not unusual to find litters of adorable puppies, as well as various older sheepdogs kept as pets, around the place. All were delivered and reared by Heather, the original pedigreed bitch from Kalamazoo, seen here in 1967.*

around to enjoy Trouble and her son, and to experience Mom and Dad's first delvings into the world of dog breeding with the purchase from Kalamazoo of Heather, a pedigreed Old English sheepdog. This sheepdog business was a warm and interesting enterprise to watch from the periphery whenever I was home from college, and later, married and on leave from the Navy.

Maple Hill Farm shared another feature with most farms back then, and that was the proliferation of semi-wild barn cats, a fluctuating population depleted by "natural" mortality and supplanted by new litters as well as animals "dropped off" by people tired of or unwilling to take care of their own pets. At times I'm certain there were at least twenty barn cats, perhaps more, around at any given time. These cats led a rough life, innocent of vaccinations, neutering, and veterinary care of any type. But in exchange for keeping the farm virtually free of rats and mice, they got to sleep in the barn, help themselves to bottomless pans of warm fresh milk, and get occasional scraps from both my aunts' and our kitchens. Kind Aunt Annie took the most interest in their welfare, naming favorites, deliberately saving scraps for them, and actually allowing a few inside. By the time dry cat food became popular, there were fewer barn cats, and in her last years Aunt Annie improved their diets considerably with the addition of this affordable and nourishing commodity.

We all got to know the old veteran survivors, like all-black, wide-faced Panther, black-and-brown mottled Ham and Eggs, Slim, and others. The litters of kittens were of course irresistible to us kids, but because distemper was epidemic, the adorable little bright-eyed fuzzballs with tails straight in the air one day might be rasping sacks of bones, eyes nearly shut by encrusted fluids, a few weeks later, then disappear. When an older cat got sick or injured to the point of obvious suffering, Father would take it out behind the barn and quickly end its agony with his .22. Then he'd bury it without ceremony.

When table scraps were scarce, my sister, Linda, would mix white bread with milk for the beggars assembled outside our kitchen door in the upstairs back shed. To accommodate more cats, she took to broadcasting this slop across the wood floor where it was eagerly licked up, resulting in a mysterious, slick surface on the floor. The mystery and the practice came to an end when, ascending the stairs, my father received a face full of the splattering liquid. From then on Linda confined her serving to dishes and pans.

I was nine or ten when we took in our first house cat, Minou, a longhaired black cat with white markings and whiskers amazingly similar to those of Tweety's bumbling nemesis, Sylvester. Minou led a pampered life, spayed, inoculated, fed canned cat food, and allowed to sleep inside wherever she pleased. She also was allowed out, and if it wasn't too cold spent a fair amount of time among the masses to whom she seemed indifferent and who ignored her as well.

Aunt Lydia was in charge of the poultry and kept varying numbers of laying hens, providing the family with fresh eggs and selling the surplus to neighbors. The hens were kept in either of two separate chicken coops that originally had fenced-in yards, but due to lack of maintenance the yards gradually deteriorated into disrepair and finally ruin, affording the hens a wider range to their seasonal foraging. I remember a string of mean-spirited roosters over the years that would attack and chase anyone, but especially kids whom they thought were threatening the flock.

There were also squat Muscovy ducks, mostly white or black and white, with ugly fleshy faces and wattled bills that walked around on stout legs, bodies parallel to the ground, unlike more graceful and upright breeds of duck. The drakes were especially unfriendly. Whenever approached, their crests would spread, their heads bobbing back and forth like a snake's, the normally short necks surprisingly extended. They would hiss menacingly through their open bills, their tail feathers beating back and forth horizontally. In warm weather, lacking a pond, these unattractive ducks hung out around the leaky wooden drinking trough alongside the barn where there were always puddles of foul water to splash around in. The yellow downy ducklings were another thing altogether, as appealing as could be, like the ugly duckling syndrome in reverse.

There was an experiment in raising turkeys lasting at least a couple years. Big white birds ranged the inner pasture and orchard during the day and were herded into little houses with raised wire-mesh floors in the evening to be shut in securely for the night. My one clear memory of this enterprise was of returning home from town with the family to the bizarre sight of the outsized white turkeys perched at intervals all the way up to the tops of two very tall spruce trees in the yard. These spruces were eighty or more feet in height, and what inspired these normally unadventursome, nearly flightless birds to work their way, branch by branch, up into the highest branches was never determined, and it occurred only that once. It's unlikely they sensed the Thanksgiving market was only a week or two away and that the accommodating spruces with their heavy branches represented an escape route to a safer world. The surreal image of the ungainly white turkeys swaying in the dark-swathed branches against a Payne's grey November sky will always be etched into my memory. Just before dark, the turkeys reconsidered their situation and on their own accord hopped back down level by level, finally assembling unscathed at the bases of the two trees and returning voluntarily to their enclosures.

From time to time there would be a pig or two kept at the farm. But as cute as piglets can be, and as likeable as even adult pigs are, knowing what fate had in store for them prevented us from getting too attached. When their time came, they were shuttled off to the slaughterhouse where the meat was processed. We might keep a smoked ham or side of bacon from one of our pigs, but usually my grandfather peddled the fresh pork to his customers in town. One reason we kept so little was that we didn't own a deep freezer. Occasionally, if it were late fall or winter, a side of pork might be safely hung alongside a deer in the unheated "old milk room."

Someone once gave my father a goat "for the kids." Nanny goat was a recalcitrant beast, all white, horns intact, that refused to stay outdoors even during the finest summer weather. She would always find a way to break free whenever staked outside, and even if the succulent green grass reached up to her knobby knees, she would run back into the barn to munch away on last year's dried-out hay.

Besides Yogi the woodchuck, we enjoyed the company of Jackie the flying squirrel for several years. This beady-eyed jokester enjoyed being tossed across the living room over and over again to glide to a smooth landing on the couch, and was not above stealing treats such as a candy bar right out of one's hand. Being nocturnal, Jackie spent most of the day sleeping and Dad would sometimes carry him around, sleeping in his shirt pocket. Sometimes when Dad was in a store or at a gas station, Jackie would awaken and stick his head out, much to the surprise of anyone who happened to be around. His vigorous nighttime use of a squeaky exercise wheel in his cage eventually became quite disruptive to my parents' sleep and as a last resort Dad was forced to wedge the wheel at night so it wouldn't turn. Jackie died, for whatever reason, a few weeks later, and my father always blamed himself for his little friend's death.

Nemo the red squirrel, a refugee from an airplane hangar at Brunswick Naval Air Station, was a delightful pet for almost a decade, and especially loved Linda. Unfortunately his temperament inexplicably took a turn for

*Linda and Nemo the red squirrel. Nemo came to her as a baby from a warehouse in Brunswick that was being cleaned out, and Linda kept him for many years. Near the end, Nemo became very cranky and it was a challenge just to clean out his cage.*

the worse after all those contented years and he became a vicious monster whenever let out of his cage, scolding, tail bristling, and teeth chattering, before launching himself at anyone within range. It reached the point where Linda had to gear up like a keeper of giant killer bees whenever she let Nemo out to clean his cage.

Each of these creatures added a dimension of diversity as well as warmth to life on the farm, although few of them added much of anything to the farm's prosperity. They were unforgettable and I am indebted to them all for their companionship and for the lessons of life and of death that resulted from their presence.

# CHAPTER SEVEN

## FROM WARM BLOOD TO COLD STEEL

When Dad took over the farm in 1960, things began happening fast—at least compared to the stagnation that characterized the operation over the previous thirty years. With the extra money he borrowed, he bought the farm's first tractors: two late-model Farmalls—a Super C and a larger Super H. The big tractor came with a bucket loader and a trailer-style mowing machine with a seven-foot bar. With the bucket Dad would be able to move the mountain of manure that had been growing in the cavernous keep beneath the cow barn. For years, he had little but a four-tined manure fork and the horse-drawn spreader with which to attack it. Removing this steaming mass would simplify cleaning out the cow stalls in the winter and benefit the undernourished hayfields.

We were all excited the day the man from Delekto Brothers trucked the Farmalls, chained onto a big trailer, to Maple Hill Farm. Although not brand-new, they were in excellent condition, spotless, and represented a long-overdue step into modern farming. The Super H was especially impressive, a good deal taller than I was, shining bright red in

*Dad and the "jitney" in 1959. This was a homebuilt tractor of sorts given to him by a neighbor. It was useful for plowing snow and hauling up the tong-like hay fork used for unloading loose hay from the hayrack or from the truck in the barn.*

the sunlight, with the lettering in bold white. The big rear tires were rimmed with capable-looking solid rubber cleats for traction. Still, they represented a bit of a compromise with the small front wheels mounted close together beneath the front end like a tricycle instead of the more stable wide-stance configuration. This made some sense because both tractors would be used some in cultivating row crops as well as in open fields; but it made them dangerous on steep-sloping land, and all but useless in the woods. They also lacked "live power," making it less convenient to operate various machines, such as a baler, off the power take off. Still, it was a lot less inconvenient than what Dad was used to, which was no auxiliary power at all, save the steady plodding strength of Buck and Don, the faithful draft horses.

Buck and Don were purchased as a team before I was born. They were "green broke," meaning they still needed training before they could be depended upon to manage all the tasks that would be demanded of them. They must have learned rapidly, because from the time of my earliest memories, Buck and Don appeared to be veterans, whether performing heavy work, such as pulling the hay mower or woods scoot, or lighter tasks, such as drawing a disk harrow or hayrake.

The two gelded strawberry roans looked enough alike to confuse strangers, but even at a distance we kids could tell them apart in an instant. What impressed me most, besides their size, were their long, Roman-nosed faces with white blazes running down between their kind and intelligent brown eyes. The size of their hooves was truly astonishing, fanning out impressively from their silky tufted fetlocks. We listened to Dad when he cautioned us not to get directly behind the gentle behemoths, because a kick could easily be fatal.

Apparently, when the horses had first arrived, their coats were mostly reddish-brown, sometimes called sorrel. But this red was not a uniform color; rather, it was spattered with tiny dots of white or light gray that seemed to increase in density as the team grew older. By the time I remember them clearly, this roan characteristic had advanced appreciably. The original sorrel was dominant only on their faces, their lower sides, and their legs above the knees. The reddish highlights showed best in bright sunlight. In flat light the pair appeared mostly light gray. In any light their glossy manes, tails, and fetlocks glistened a silvery white. Their nearly black muzzles were velvet smooth, and their lips rubbery. You kept your hand flat when you fed an apple or a lump of sugar to Buck or Don.

Buck and Don spent much of their time tethered by longish ropes in partitioned box stalls across from the cow barn, patiently awaiting their next outing. They had prodigious appetites, grazing all day long when out to pasture or indoors munching down hay half a bale at a time, followed by ten gallons or so of water. When they were working hard, they were fed protein-enriched grain with lots of oats that smelled good, and tasted good, too.

Their first work in the spring, once the fields dried, was drawing a classic old-fashioned plow to turn the soil over in the tomato patch and family vegetable gardens, plus any plot that would be devoted that year to sweet corn. My father stumped along behind on the uneven earth, guiding the plow by its wooden handles, the long reins tossed loosely over his back. Later they'd drag the disk harrow over the newly turned earth to bust up and flatten the furrows—relatively light work for them.

By contrast, mowing tall, thick hay with a metal-wheeled mechanical mowing machine can be hot, hard work for both horses and operator. Round and round the often uneven fields under the hot morning sun, Buck and Don drew this ponderous machine. The razor-sharp triangular teeth, riveted to a bar, scissored back and forth, cleaving off timothy and clover alike as it was parted by the advancing comb-like fingers that moved steadily through the crop and laid the shorn hay behind. From the cast-metal seat between the wheels Dad scanned the ground immediately ahead for rocks, branches, and similar obstacles, or even a huddled clutch of young hares, ready to raise the bar at an instant's notice by means of a frayed line. But everything was not seen in time and sometimes the hay was just too thick and tall, clogging the reciprocating bar. Then Dad, coppery skin the color of a summer deer, would be forced to halt the operation. The horses stopped, Dad would climb down and clear whatever was jamming the sickle bar, or move any obstructions. Then he'd remount the machine, back up the team a few feet, engage the mechanism, and proceed. A six- or seven-acre plot of fragrant hay laying evenly and drying in a parquet pattern represents a minor triumph, combining the muscle and training of a good team with the skill, patience, and endurance of the operator. Dad was a good mower. He mowed a field cleanly, seldom damaged the equipment, and treated Buck and Don with consideration and respect, resting them frequently in the shade at the end of the field. He was a master of an art that even back then was already out of date.

Compared with mowing, raking the hay represented relatively easy work. The wide big-wheeled dump rake first dragged the dried hay into windrows, and then by straddling the windrows gathered them into bunches that simplified the process of pitching the loose hay onto the wagon. A row of curved springy tines set aft of the axle provided the raking action. When a lever was pulled, the spring-loaded tines were

118

*Gentle giants Buck and Don got welcomed respites in the pasture once the haying was completed and before woods work began in the winter. Here, in 1959, they dwarf Linda, who no doubt had just brought them carrots or apples.*

lifted clear of the hay, depositing the accumulated load at that spot. It took many passes in a crisscross pattern to get the job done and the light rig was pulled by just one horse between traces. My grandfather normally performed this task, with Don providing the power. Poor, easy-natured Don was always the horse called upon for jobs requiring just one of the team. More temperamental, Buck pulled hard enough and behaved well when harnessed next to his teammate, but never got used to working alone. If hitched solo to any implement, he would do his best to kick it apart. It was also Don's broad back that Dad would mount for a ride when taking the team down to the lower woodlot or over to the "seventeen-acre" field on the Beaver Road that measured closer to thirteen acres.

When Buck and Don set out to work in any season they were not decked out in gorgeous harness gear like the Budweiser Clydesdales. Their black leather harnesses were simple and had been repaired often, the leather dull and seldom oiled. The chains and metal fittings were rusted, the whiffletrees and doubletree were of checked, weathered wood, the blue-painted hames faded. The excelsior padding in the leather chafing collars sprang out from cracks. My grandfather kept this shabby gear sound, replacing and adding straps and rivets as needed, but he paid little attention to detail and was not one much for show. Gran'pa likewise trimmed the team's feet and replaced horseshoes after having a blacksmith in Lewiston form them to a pattern. He enjoyed working with metal, and with few proper tools and only a little brass blowtorch was often found heating iron to a bright cherry red and forming it into eye straps or similar fittings to replace something on the truck bed, scoot, or hayrack.

I don't recall Buck or Don experiencing any problems with their hooves. For that matter, I don't believe either horse ever required the services of a veterinarian or missed a day's work because of a health-related problem. Any sores or minor cuts were treated with Rawleigh's ointment. Lameness and muscle soreness responded well to a rubbing with liniment.

Maple Hill Farm included two woodlots: one of about sixty acres down beyond the field across the road, and another of forty-five acres out back. From them Dad and Gran'pa cut cords of firewood for the house, and many winters pulpwood and saw logs to generate some much-needed cash. Wintertime, when the ground was frozen and snow-covered was the season for this strenuous activity, and the means of transporting the wood out of the lot was a heavy

121

horse-drawn sledge called a "scoot." Built by Gran'pa, its runners were solid red oak, about four inches thick, a foot wide, and a dozen feet long. The cribwork carriage was mounted over these runners by bolted iron straps and angled irons. On rough ground, heavily loaded, the whole rig creaked and swayed a bit, and this small margin of flexibility probably is what kept the scoot from breaking apart. Four-foot pulpwood and firewood was piled across the carriage between pairs of stakes, fore and aft. Dad loaded this four-foot wood by hand using a pulp hook and sometimes a peavey or cantdog. Two or three, or sometimes more, big saw logs would be rolled up onto the carriage lengthwise by Dad and Gran'pa using cantdogs and rough poles for ramps. The logs were prevented from rolling off by three pairs of stakes along the sides.

When the school bus dropped us off on a sunny winter day it didn't take long for Henry Lewis and me to follow the double runner tracks down to the yarding area of whichever woodlot was being worked. There we'd find Dad bucking up some small logs into pulpwood with his huge temperamental chainsaw that belched a thick blue cloud of oily smoke as it roared deafeningly. Helping him might be Gran'pa or Donnie Lyons from up the road, who worked off and on for Dad after returning from Korea. Hitched to the scoot, Buck and Don would be standing patiently in their traces, half dozing in the low-angled sunlight. Henry and I would play around the brush piles until it was time to take the load out, either to the farmyard or to an accessible place at the bottom of the field. Then we'd pile on, swaying with the load on the creaking carriage as the runners sluiced along the trail through the late-season corn snow. Dad stood at the reins, and ahead of him the powerful haunches of Buck and Don worked like pistons, their long tails swishing back and forth, their mighty hooves splattering slush and mud, their alert heads swinging side to side, almost in rhythm.

Once the horses were sold, we had no means of getting logs out of the woodlot. Surely, the foolish tractors couldn't do it. From time to time Dad would sell the stumpage off a section of a lot to a woods operator who cut and yarded the logs for a modest profit. Most of our firewood, save a few cords cut each year along the stone walls, we ended up buying.

I won't forget the afternoon I stepped off the school bus and saw a truck with high sideboards backed up to the barn. The loading ramp was just being raised and latched. On the truck bed stood Buck and Don, hitched facing backwards, their heads and shoulders above the sides and their ears back, no doubt wondering what was going on. I ran past, into the shed and up the back stairs. Without it ever being mentioned in my presence, I knew that this was going to happen. Still, I wasn't prepared for the reality of the parting. Inside, Mother, looking nervous, stood at the kitchen window looking down into the yard where my father and grandfather stood talking with the man who had brought the truck. Mother snapped a picture just before the truck with our loyal and gentle friends aboard pulled out of the yard.

All at once I hated the big red tractors that sat smugly under the trees, and would gladly have done without them if only Buck and Don, then nearly twenty years old, could have remained on the farm.

Easy for me to say. My father no doubt felt the saddest of all. But he had a farm to run, and it was already thirty years behind the times, with him having to make up the difference by working twice as hard. And we could ill afford to keep two idle horses around that ate two or three times as much each day as a milk cow.

Buck and Don were sold to a woods operator who ran a logging camp up by The Forks. He still preferred horses to bulldozers for some jobs, and had a reputation for taking proper care of his teams. And they would get their summers off. Buck and Don still had some good years in their legs, and I like to think they adjusted to their new vastly different circumstances. But I'm convinced they must have thought back to their lives at Maple Hill Farm and to their pastures with its shade trees and abundant green grass. Did they miss the routine of seasonal work that, although sometimes hard, was seldom boring or prolonged?

I know Dad thought about them from time to time. And even years later he regretted that he was unable to keep those handsome and gentle creatures, just to have them around the farm, enjoying a well-earned retirement in a familiar environment.

# Chapter Eight

## Summertime!
## And the Living's Not So Easy

The long, steamy, hot days of summer were not a time for being lazy. It was a time when extra money could be made with a good early crop of tomatoes, and the winter's hay—enough to feed forty head of cattle and the work horses—had to be put in the barn.

Because Maple Hill was on high ground, we faced less chance of a late spring frost damaging the new plants than farms in the valleys. Lacking a greenhouse of our own, Dad and Gran'pa each had about 1,500 seedlings started in March at a local grower's. As soon as the May full moon began waning it was time to get them planted in the traditional plot that always seemed to dry out sufficiently in time.

Dad planted most of the seedlings by hand with Gran'pa and sometimes Aunt Lydia helping out. Once set in the ground, each plant got a soup can's worth of water, likely the only moisture other than precipitation it would receive in its short life. After a week or so to "harden" in the ground, especially if rain was forecast, a ring of a commercial fertilizer was spilled around each plant, and a small mound of soil hoed up around it. The concept of organic farming was still many years in the future, but with our tomatoes it wasn't a big issue. Nearly every plant survived and thrived. The only pest worth bothering with was a cutworm, which was kept under control by a single dusting of a suffocating agent such as rotenone.

By the time school let out for summer vacation in mid-June, the plants in these seemingly endless rows were already struggling to stay ahead of the weeds and witch grass. Linda and I commonly spent our weekday mornings pulling these resilient intruders out by their roots, being careful not to disturb the plants. This was dusty work, done on our hands and knees, slowly working our way up the two-hundred-foot rows. We'd try keeping pace with one another so we could talk or even sing songs to make the time, which always seemed to be seriously dragging, go by. Once we'd finished Dad's dozen or so rows over a period of a couple weeks, we spent a few days pulling the weeds in the family garden, after which it was time to return to the dreaded tomatoes, already beset by a new generation of thicker and tougher weeds.

As I got older I learned to chop the weeds between plants and build up the protective mounds with a hoe. Early in the summer the wide paths between rows could be controlled with the spring-tooth harrow or cultivator pulled by Don, the draft horse, and later by a tractor. But because our tomato plants were not staked, they had a tendency to spread outward, and by July the tendrils of the plants within a given row began to entwine and snake their way out into the pathways, making them ever narrower. Eventually Dad purchased a big front-tined rototiller to clear what was left of the paths. This was not a smooth-running machine, and you got a good workout guiding the beast as it bucked like a mule bitten by wasps.

By the third week in July there would be ripe tomatoes—large firm fruit, yet juicy, with a distinctive sweet taste—several weeks ahead of most of the competitors. Gran'pa, a good peddler anyway, had no trouble selling all he had to stands and supermarkets for the unheard-of price of up to thirty-five cents a pound.

A patch of grass between the house and tomato patch became the staging area. There, Dad carefully emptied the buckets of fruit, and Aunts Lydia and Annie and Mother

*Tomatoes grew well at Maple Hill Farm. They ripened early, were famous for their flavor, and became the principal crop raised for market. Here, in 1950, a day's picking is being sorted and packed by Dad, Mother, and Aunt Helen.*

sorted the tomatoes, polished them, and carefully set them into half-bushel wooden boxes. If the weather turned sour or darkness fell, the operation was relocated into the dismal shed between the ell and the barn, and the packing was completed in the light cast from a pair of weak light bulbs. In the morning Gran'pa loaded the boxes onto the bed of his ancient truck and started his rounds to potential buyers.

By early August other farmers' crops started to ripen. Our own yield was by now prodigious and the picking and packing operations sometimes went on all day, with Aunt Helen from down the road joining the team spread out between the piles of tomatoes. Naturally this abundance was accompanied by a dramatic drop in the price: down to twenty, then fifteen and ten cents a pound. Even then Gran'pa had to work hard to sell each day's output. When the price dropped to five cents a pound we began selling perfectly beautiful tomatoes for canning for a few dollars a bushel. People from town drove out to our place to get a bushel or two to be put up as stewed tomatoes and sauces. Residents of towns as far north of us as Strong and Rangeley drove down each season to get their tomatoes, probably because back then there were few hardy varieties available. Still, the size of the crop began outstripping our ability to harvest it and we opened the field to eager customers who enjoyed picking their own canners for two dollars a bushel. Years after Dad had stopped growing commercially, old customers from all over would show up at our place in late September, hoping for a chance to get a few bushels of these beautiful tomatoes.

The competing interests of growing tomatoes and harvesting our hay crop for the winter were often at odds with one another, and around mid-July the two disparate activities began overlapping, if not actually colliding. Largely because of time spent getting the tomato crop off to a good start we seldom began haying before July 1, when many farms were already completing their first crops. Our outdated methods were another reason our haying season lasted nearly the entire summer. Until 1960 all the hay was mowed by Dad using Buck and Don, raked into bunches by the old dump rake, and then pitched by hand onto a long, narrow wagon called the hayrack. This horse-drawn, open-framed wagon had large iron wheels with a narrow body that extended out over the wheels with two-foot-wide shelves that made it possible to build a wide load of interwoven loose hay. When I was about ten, this antique was replaced by a farm truck of a couple tons with a wooden bed fitted with a headboard and sideboards. Up until then most of the "tramping" and load-building had been done by Cousin Arnie with Dad and Gran'pa pitching on the hay. Known for his stamina and strength, Dad on occasion speared so much hay with his fork that the long handle would break with a loud snap as he swung it up and over his head, causing Gran'pa to swear and shake his head because he would have to make or buy a new handle and install it.

For a few summers, my pal, Joe Tomlinson, helped me tramp down the hay and build the load as it came aboard the truck. We each had pitchforks with shorter handles, with which we could intercept forkfuls coming aboard and help pull them up and place the hay for a wide, secure load. We kept faith in our work as we worked ever closer to the edge as the load grew taller, actually extending a good deal beyond the now-invisible sideboards.

Dad drove the loaded truck to the barn, with us sitting on the soft yet prickly load. Joe and I would run upstairs for Kool-Aid and water while Dad positioned the load beneath an opening between the two scaffolds fifteen feet above. A double-tonged fork resembling a great spider was rigged onto a track that ran beneath the ridgepole of the barn an additional fifteen feet above the scaffolds. It was hinged and designed to grapple a huge clump of hay from the load and, through a series of pulleys and sheaves, lift the bunch up to the peak, where it ran along the lofty track until it was stopped in a good position to drop its load onto the scaffold. The power at one end was provided by Don, the draft horse, whose whiffletree was hitched to a rope of great length. He was guided by Gran'pa, walking him out toward the road. The fork's travel along the track and its descent, ascent, and dumping were controlled by my father, who intercepted the huge steel "hay fork" as it descended and set it into the load by opening it to its full breadth and standing on it, to get it to bite. The interlocking properties of loose hay were normally enough to hold the bunch together and the tong-like hooks held as long as tension was maintained. Still, lots of loose hay, as well as a shower of itchy chaff, rained down on Dad, sticking to his sweaty skin. He took care to be standing clear when the rising fork hit the track overhead because, once in awhile, that was enough of a jolt to send the whole clump tumbling down, which could easily have buried if not actually crushed him. We'd signal Gran'pa to stop Don when the loaded fork was positioned, and Dad could trip the mechanism with yet another line. In this ingenious way, untold tons of hay were piled onto the lofty scaffolds. Eventually, usually on rainy days, it had to be pitched down onto the lower mows alongside to make room for more hay.

By the time we had the tractors, and soon afterward a green John Deere baler and side delivery rake, I was getting old enough for serious work. Dad continued to do all the mowing with the trailer mower behind the big tractor. He might let me kick up the hay with the tedder, to promote faster drying. Normally with good drying conditions, the

*Dad, in the later stages of farming in 1992, tows the John Deere baler with his Farmall Super H across the road from the farm buildings. After years of dairy and beef-cattle farming, Dad kept around a few head that needed to be provided for.*

hay cut the previous day would be ready for Dad to rake into windrows before lunch. Right after, he'd begin baling.

Besides me, the haying crew now included Henry Lewis, who for some reason preferred working on the farm to hanging around the Taylor Pond Yacht Club, plus Harold Walker, cousin Mike, and Gran'pa to drive the big truck, whose flat bed no longer needed the side boards. As Gran'pa drove slowly along between the rows of bales, two of us boys would gather the bales and with a boost from our thighs throw them up onto the bed, where the third and sometimes fourth crewmember piled them into nine-bale tiers. Not infrequently on some of the more hilly fields Gran'pa would release the clutch a bit too quickly, jerking the truck and starting the tiers of bales toppling backward like dominoes. Usually the stacker was nimble enough to jump clear and not be swept off along with most of the load.

Eventually, we'd tie off the sixty-three-bale load and climb on top for the ride back to the barn. On the remote fields this might be a forty-mile-an-hour drive along the lane-like roads. We reveled in the cool breeze, getting slapped by boughs of leaves, and ducking the larger limbs that might easily have knocked someone foolish and swept him off the end of the load onto the tarmac.

Back at the barn, Henry would take over from Gran'pa, backing the loaded truck up to the portable conveyor-style elevator that had replaced the big tongs as the means for moving the hay up into the lofts. One of us would feed bales onto the conveyor while the other two, up in the sweltering dusty mow, stacked them. For me, constantly afflicted with hay fever or similar allergies, this was the worst part, and I spent a part of most afternoons with runny eyes and nose, sneezing continuously and at times struggling for breath. In those days this was considered an acceptable inconvenience, and medication, dust masks, or simply not haying were never even considered. In this way, between milking and other chores, letting the cows in and out, and picking tomatoes, we'd put up three hundred bales on a typical day.

Happily, our summers were more than just work. The long evenings were perfect for playing whiffleball (there were never enough of us around to play baseball), riding bikes, or fooling around. We'd climb up into one of the prolific cherry trees when the fruit ripened, eating our fill alongside the robins, after Mother had picked all she was planning to can for the winter. Green apples were another summer treat. We'd borrow the big green salt shaker from the downstairs dining room and climb up into any of a score of apple trees and eat as many, covered with a layer of salt, as we cared to without ever getting the threatened bellyaches.

Sometimes there were visitors, usually relatives from Massachusetts, our favorites being Dad's Aunt Stella, her husband, Sam, and their daughter, Marilyn. While Aunt

Stella visited, Sam helped out haying or in the garden and before chores added a little festivity to the operation for the adults with his frosty green bottles of Ballantine Ale. Poker games went on every night when Sam and Stella were around, and Marilyn, and her cousin, Ruthie, older than the rest of us, would take us kids swimming at Bear Pond, where there was also a sorry little amusement park. On Sunday, everybody would pack up and cram into several cars and go to Sebago State Park or Old Orchard Beach as a group.

Traveling was never an option for us with all the work that needed doing, daily chores, and milking. But each year as the summer progressed our family would plan a week's worth of daytrips we'd hope to take before school started after Labor Day. Destinations included Old Orchard Beach and Reid State Park on the coast, Rangeley inland, and perhaps one or two of the early agricultural fairs. In reality we seldom managed to accomplish even this modest itinerary, and with haying dragging on right up until summer's end, we'd wind up settling for two or three of our choices.

Old Orchard Beach, with its miles of white sand beaches, amusement park, and concession pier, was our favorite, and I'd usually bring along Joe. Linda would invite Marilyn Davenport or another pal. At summer's end the place would be mobbed. In those days Old Orchard was an annual vacation destination for thousands of French-Canadians from Québec City and Montréal, and it seemed there was as much French as English spoken. Adults and children alike played in the big translucent-green breakers rolling in on the beach. And there were vacationers showing a lot more deeply tanned skin than we were accustomed to as they reclined on their lounges or sprawled on blankets and colorful beach towels.

Mother and Dad would lie in the sun and we'd head down to the water's edge where you were necessarily shoulder-to-shoulder with other romping bathers. Until I was ten or eleven, all it took was a sideward look or a playful splash from any of the noisier, more aggressive kids and I was out of the water and back up on the blanket with my parents.

The pier and amusements were the real destination. Supported by bundles of huge pilings, the pier jutted boldly out into the open Atlantic for what seemed like a hundred yards. Back when my parents were dating there was a big dance pavilion at the seaward end where they went to listen and dance to the big swing bands of the era. But by this time the pavilion had been gone for years, swept away in a fierce ocean storm. Most of the rides and other amusements were clustered at the pier's base, and early in the afternoon that's where we would head. Above the colorful dense crowd loomed the regal Ferris wheel and the modest roller coaster.

There was a bizarre funhouse named Noah's Ark, distinguished by a surreal representation of the vessel rocking on its cradle high above everything near it. From its deck and portholes peered an assortment of improbable animals, clowns, and other colorful wacky figures, larger than life.

We ate slices of thin greasy pizza and French fries sprinkled with vinegar, always tossing some to the bold seagulls that mewed and flashed just above the surging swells. We'd split up and take our time making our way out to the end past concessions, arcades, shooting galleries, and souvenir shops. Joe and I would go on a ride or two, and along with Linda and Marilyn, brave Noah's Ark with the hall of mirrors, huge, slowly rotating barrel, and scary surprises deep in its recesses. I'd take such a beating on the bumper cars that eventually the more adept young drivers tired of ramming into me and left me alone. Linda would buy a souvenir or two, and before we knew it the afternoon would be spent. We'd walk back to the parking lot, tired and thankful for the rest provided by the ride home, where we'd arrive to get a late start letting in the cows and doing the chores.

In 1956 or so my parents purchased a small lot on Sandy Bottom Pond about five miles from Maple Hill in the neighboring town of Turner. Sandy Bottom is half a mile long and a couple hundred yards wide. It is only about fifteen feet deep and is spring-fed. There were about a dozen developed lots at one end, extending up along one shore, and a sandy public beach at the other.

Our wooded lot rose up a steep bank from the fifty-foot frontage to the dirt road, and Dad's first job was to cut a switchback trail down to the water, cutting in steps at the corners. At the water's edge he cut down most of the trees, leaving a few nice maples and a pine tree or two for shade, then removing the mat-like surface duff and roots to reveal the fine-sand deposit for which the pond was named. It was then a matter of transferring the sand into the water and a cut-in beach began to grow. Dad accomplished most of this work Sundays and evenings, and in retrospect I realize it represented a good deal of work for someone doing chores seven days a week and farming all week long. Eventually the water's edge, as well as the embankment, were stabilized by stacked logs set in and backfilled with small rocks, soil, and finally sand.

The following year, Frank and Catherine Volock, distant relatives, bought a lot on Sandy Bottom; a fallow lot between us belonging to out-of-staters was never improved or used, affording a nice woodsy buffer and a private pathway between properties. Cousins Bob and Arlene were just our ages, and with lots of common interests, we now had great companions whenever we visited the pond, which was mostly on Sundays. There were frequent family cookouts, and these modest retreats on this pretty little pond proved surprisingly popular.

We all learned to swim at Sandy Bottom, me last of all, and the spring-fed water stayed refreshingly cool all summer long. Soon, both families had wooden skiffs, ours a nice-looking heavy-duty model built by our neighbors on the hill, the Davenports. I don't remember whether Dad actually bought the boat or we had it on rather permanent loan. But I know each season, once we recaulked the cross-bottom seams and painted it, the skiff sat at our dock all summer, leaking very little.

The pond was home to a small population of painted turtles, and Bob and I stalked them relentlessly. The turtles would be sunning themselves on limbs of fallen trees sticking out of the water, and it didn't take much to get them to plop off into the pond and escape. I'd row slowly past a potential catch at a respectable distance, and Bob would slide into the water, approach the terrapin underwater using a snorkel, and, if lucky, grab it. We'd take the captive back to shore and once its carapace dried paint an identifying number on it with durable yellow enamel paint. Once the paint dried, it was released. Needless to say, a few of those turtles

*Cousin Bob Volock at Sandy Bottom in 1960 with a bullfrog we'd caught so often it became quite tame. The Volocks bought the next lot over from ours, and the kids, Arlene and Bob, shared many interests with Linda and me.*

became very familiar, as they were caught over and over. The shores were also home to water snakes that sent the girls splashing noisily ashore whenever one slithered by on the surface. There were also huge ugly spiders living under the docks. And I'm ashamed to say, they became targets for our BB guns whenever they ventured out to sun themselves on the retaining logs.

Eventually the Volocks built a cabin halfway up on the wooded hillside, where they frequently stayed over. Through one of his woodlot deals, Dad obtained a neat two-room camp that we had moved to our lot and set on posts. Because we were only five miles from home, and the cows needed milking twice each day, we never stayed over at our camp and used it only as a refuge when a Sunday outing was interrupted by rain.

Two events associated with Sandy Bottom stand out from the many pleasant memories as being more or less life-changing. The first was our discovery of chain pickerel in the pond. These backstreet brawlers of the pike family would lie stock-still beneath sunken trees and charge out and slam into our red and white Daredevle lures. Once hooked, they slugged it out with determination and endurance and provided our first thrills battling strong fish. They were unsophisticated enough for us to outsmart and these pickerel whet both Bob's appetite and mine, launching in both of us a lifelong passion for fishing.

One evening a year or two later, I was standing on the shore and across the little pond the quiet surface was disturbed, just barely, by a vision of grace and beauty that I would never forget. Parting the water almost silently, propelled by a quickly flashing paddle, was a lovely wooden canoe—this one an Old Town with fully curved stems, a subtle but proud sheerline, and white painted canvas decorated with an "Indian" pattern of red and blue triangles along the sheer. I watched the canoe gliding across the surface, its perfect reflection keeping apace. Then I looked down rather critically at the fine, trusty old rowboat that had served me so well and I knew intuitively that nothing would ever be the same.

# CHAPTER NINE

## AUTUMN'S MESSAGE:
## ANT OR GRASSHOPPER?

Autumn in Maine often provides the finest weather of the year, and it can also be the most diverse. Some years, September will run along for half its length as an extension of the summer, yet by late November the wind can come howling out of the north, swirling before it snow that is here to stay until spring. Autumn also marks the start of the school year, and many years the work at school and that of summer overlapped. When the summer weather had been particularly unfavorable for making hay, we might still be putting up less-than-prime hay right into September. I would get off the small school bus, really just a yellow panel truck, around three in the afternoon and help with a load or two of hay before chores and supper.

The cows were still let out to pasture each day, but by mid-September they were kept inside nights. By mid-October they were in for the winter—tied at their stalls, where they could either stand or lie down—and seemed perfectly content with the limited circumstances.

Hard frosts came late to Maple Hill and there were tomatoes to pick throughout September into early October—mostly canning tomatoes. On weekends especially there were always customers driving out to pick their own. There was still plenty of sweet corn, but that was mostly for our own consumption—ours and the raccoons'. During my earliest years this was not the case, and a lot of sweet corn was raised for market, including for the small seasonal canning facility in North Auburn village at the foot of the hill. Some years there were potatoes to sell but never on a large scale. Other years it might be cabbages. One October the deer developed a great appetite for cabbage, although it was a crop they had never before bothered. The cabbages were raised alongside the tomato patch behind the house, and at night you could hear the deer noisily munching on the heads. If you shined a flashlight beam out the window it would reflect back a half dozen pairs of bright eyes, as the deer paused just long enough from their dinner to look up. It got so bad that Dad obtained a permit and for the first and only time took a deer in the name of crop protection. A few days later the crop was sold and that was the end of the problem.

As I've mentioned, Maple Hill Farm had once been a small commercial orchard, and even though scores of trees had been taken down over the years to make space for dairying and raising crops, there were still thirty or so that regularly bore fruit. Most of these were located in the pasture alongside the barn. From late August until freeze-up these untended trees provided a variety of apples for our own use, including Mother's perfect pies. The drops, if not occurring all at once, made a welcome addition to the cows' diets as well. Among my favorites were the Wealthies—medium-sized, sweet, and juicy—but you wanted to eat them fresh off the tree. There was also a variety of large yellow-green apple with a blush that ripened early and was so huge you needed both hands to hold one to your mouth. Down across the road by the stone wall stood a couple McIntosh apple trees whose fruit went mostly to the birds until the wind shook them down and they were gobbled down by the heifers pastured there. In addition, there were Northern Spies, Baldwin's, Black Oxfords, and other varieties that kept well over the winter, although we seldom took advantage of this important property. We did gather some of the later varieties, filling burlap grain sacks with fruit we shook down from the trees using a pole with a hook at one end. Sadly, we didn't own a cider press, and Gran'pa would sell them to a processor.

It is a testament to the hardiness of these neglected trees and the quality of the soil that they continued producing good crops most years without the benefits of pruning and spraying. As the years passed, the yield dwindled along with the quality of the apples, which got smaller, knobbier, and increasingly susceptible to scale and fruit worms. As trees died, usually due to winterkill, they were cut down without ceremony or regret, and their limbs and trunks added to the woodpile.

Cutting firewood and tossing it into the woodshed became a serious endeavor as autumn marched along, because we never seemed to have a supply of firewood cut, split, and drying a year or even six months ahead. Some years, behind the barn there would be a stack of four-foot hardwood that had been harvested during the previous winter's woods work. This was rendered into stove-length firewood by a stationary saw rig powered by one of the tractors, and before that by an old make-or-break donkey engine. At one end of the shaft turned an unguarded circular blade about a yard in diameter, driven by a wide and very worn leather belt running to the power source. On the saw frame was a hinged shelf with a fence onto which a single log of up to eight or nine inches in diameter or several smaller sticks, could be set. The operator tilted this shelf into the whirring blade, which handily cut the wood to the specified length. It was not a quiet operation and the screeching saw running through the wood drowned out the tractor noise and propelled a jet of sawdust downward like sparks from a grinder. My job after school would be to hold onto the short, soon-to-be-severed ends as Dad pushed the wood on the shelf through the saw blade. Once the pieces were lopped off I'd toss them into the back of the truck instead of letting them fall to the ground. You paid attention each time your hands traveled past, within a foot of the intimidating, hungry blade, and it was one job that managed to suppress my normally wandering imagination. Years later, reading Robert Frost's starkly matter-of-fact poem "Out, Out," I was reminded of just how different things were growing up in those days.

As the September days flew by, the weather sweetened and there would be warm days, the sky bright blue with silver clouds floating overhead and ever shorter evenings with falling temperatures. The nights were crisper still with

151

stars bright as diamonds against the sky. By the start of October the mixed forests that blanketed the hills and valleys alike were coming into their own in terms of fall color. The plentiful maples kicked the whole thing off with the dull, late-summer leaves bursting into every shade of yellow, orange, and scarlet. Soon the birch, aspen, beech, and oak trees added their own particular hues to the palette, and the whole montage was punctuated by the dark forest green of the spruce, fir, and white pine. Wild creatures increased their activity, the foxes on the move, busily hunting mice, and the deer coming out earlier to the edges of the fields. We'd stop whatever we were doing when we detected the first cronks of high-flying geese, which were rare in those days, to watch and listen spellbound as a ragged wedge of the long-necked birds passed overhead on its way south.

Sunday, especially in the fall, was the time for family drives out into the surrounding countryside, to take in the foliage and maybe buy some apple cider at a farm stand. We'd pick up Babci (Băp' chée) and Dzidzu (Jă jew), Mother's parents, who lived in Lewiston. Mikolaj and Catherine Klimek had emigrated from Poland and worked in the local textile mills most of their lives, lived on the outskirts of town, and never owned an automobile. They did own a beautifully maintained house on a double lot, and grew a fabulous garden and tended a few productive

*My mother's parents, Mikolaj and Catherine Klimek, outside their immaculate home in Lewiston in 1961. Polish immigrants, both had worked at a textile mill, but in their retirement spent lots of time and energy in the bountiful garden they maintained on their double lot in town. "Babci," as we called Catherine, was an exceptionally skilled cook of Polish dishes.*

fruit trees, including varieties of peach and plum. Babci spent many hours in late summer and fall putting up the bountiful produce from these endeavors, including making delicious preserves and pickles, all of it stored for the winter in their spotless orderly basement. She was an exceptional cook of Polish dishes, even among a large number of her skilled peers. Together, they heaped the long tables at the Polish Club on Lisbon Street with periodic feasts that were followed by dances leaning heavily to lively polkas. Dzidzu was a soft-spoken gentleman, always neat and well-dressed. He was a lapsed musician and a respectable figure in the neighborhood, as well as in the barroom and on the billiard tables at the club.

These autumn afternoon drives were preambulations often without a set destination, but they took us through the hilly rural country of towns such as Buckfield, Canton, Hebron, Paris Hill, and beyond, and by the time I was about ten years old they drove me absolutely crazy. Within a year or two I was able to argue my way out of going on these quietly social but seemingly pointless drives, not because I didn't love my grandparents, but because I was near bursting with energy. I would much rather be outside exploring in the woods or heading over to West Auburn with Joe and Henry to participate in pickup football games.

Even on the hill Joe and I embraced the featured sports of the season, but usually there were just the two of us and the rules had to be somewhat altered. With football, we'd pick two teams to represent, say, Notre Dame and Syracuse University. Representing Notre Dame we'd work our way up the field in one direction, Joe being the quarterback and me the center and receiver. Obviously there was no defense to oppose us. If we failed to reach the end of the field in a specified number of plays, we'd turn around and head downfield in the opposite direction carrying the colors of Syracuse. This system resulted in a lot of touchdowns for both teams and we found out how different things could be once we started playing against actual opposition at school and on Sundays at Hayes' in West Auburn.

Having nurtured a healthy interest in the macabre from an early age, I couldn't wait each October for the arrival of Halloween, and actually placed it right up alongside Christmas as my favorite holiday. When it came to trick-or-treating I was a purist, and so were most of my Maple Hill pals, and we insisted on making the rounds on foot, even though houses at that time averaged a quarter of a mile or so apart, there were no sidewalks or streetlights, and lots of wooded sections stood between homes. We discouraged parents from accompanying us and would rather not go at all if some overprotective mother decided she would drive us just because it was raining. It amounted to about a four- or five-mile hike for a take of treats that barely covered the bottoms of our bags. But I certainly wouldn't have traded our spooky little ventures for all the candy in the county if it had meant being driven around town.

On Maple Hill everyone knew one another, and at each house we were invited inside where the adults would try and guess who was who beneath our rather lame put-together costumes. We'd be offered glasses of cider or soda and we'd take our small handful of candy, the proffered caramel popcorn ball, or, heaven forbid, an apple, drop the treat into our bag and file back out. On dark nights between the more distant houses we'd try scaring each other with stories of mummies and werewolves, and by pointing out a dead "hangman's tree" silhouetted against a quarter moon.

One special Halloween, Dad finished chores early and hitched Buck and Don to the old hayrack. We had a huge turnout of maybe a dozen kids, and in a cold drizzle Dad patiently drove us around the hill, stopping the horses to let us off and waiting for us to emerge from the houses and climb back aboard. Mother brought along a flashlight against the unlikely event we'd encounter an automobile, but as I remember it we did not.

November can be a somber month after the bright skies and riotous colors of October. All the leaves—save those on the young beeches that hold onto theirs all winter long—have fallen weeks before. The rain-blackened skeletons of the bare hardwood trees seem to be all that are holding up the leaden sky.

Firewood continued to be a priority, since we burned many cords between the upstairs and downstairs apartments. Dad and Gran'pa always had more projects on the buildings than they could possibly attend to before winter set in.

It was also deer hunting season, and this was the one activity Dad continued to pursue despite all that needed doing. And even though most of his hunting was restricted to the hour or so around sunrise and its counterpart at sunset, more years than not, before the season was over, the winter's venison—in the form of a stiffened brown deer carcass—was hanging in the shed or from a maple limb outside. Hunting was an interest and even a passion that he managed to instill in me and it became the source of many happy hours together, close to freezing, watching a favorite

*Deer hunting was a part of every November, and venison a welcome part of most winters' diet. Here are Dad and me in 1960 with two bucks, the one on the right my first deer.*

crossing and knowing there was only a slim chance one of the hill's wary deer might actually appear.

Thanksgiving provided an opportunity for a day together with family over the traditional dinner spiced up with a few Polish dishes. But once I was old enough to carry a rifle even the afternoon football games couldn't keep us from going back out into the woods after the meal for one more chance at the elusive whitetails.

Usually by the end of November there was snow on the ground, which although not entirely welcome, at least covered up the brown bare ground. It would likely stay around until the springtime sun regained its position high in the sky, and for all practical purposes we had entered winter.

# CHAPTER TEN

## WE TAKE TO THE WOODS

The woods down behind the barn and across the road and elsewhere on Maple Hill are not vast, mysterious, or remarkable. Like mixed forests throughout central Maine they are a mix of white pine, rock maple, beech, white ash, and birch. Anchored on well-drained, gentle hillsides these woods are crisscrossed by stone walls demarking former fields wrested from the existing forest through enormous effort only to be allowed to return again to their former wooded state as Maine's and the nation's economies turned from an agricultural to an industrial base.

All but absent are swamps or marshes of any size, along with most of the diverse wildlife species associated with such wetlands. Still, from our barnyard you could strike off in almost any direction and encounter a mile or so of woodlands, in some cases having to cross an intervening road or a field or two. And this was woods enough for Joe, Henry, and me to explore while we were growing up.

My early introductions to the woods were mostly accompanying Dad, riding on the pulp scoot or mending the fences in the lower wooded pastures in late spring before the cows were let out. From his years cutting wood, hunting, and, in his youth, trapping, Dad always had stories to tell: a prize fox caught behind that stone wall, a deer killed or even missed crossing that woods road. Just as exciting to me were accounts of mere sightings of a weasel, a rare moose, or a bobcat. These were enough to stir my imagination, and before I was very old I wanted to further explore this enchanting woodscape for myself. Joe was usually more than willing to embark on these little forays that stemmed from the existing skid trails to such, in our minds, alluring destinations as "the caves," modest rocky ledges with crevices and overhangs that porcupines frequently sought out for shelter. The little spring-fed brook that swelled in the spring and ran clear over and between the rocks and boulders at the foot of the ledges became a destination in itself. By following its winding course we eventually made our way down to the foot of the hill where it flows into Lake Auburn, behind the miniature golf course at Taber's ice cream stand. Before very long, "our" woods became very familiar to us, and we could pinpoint locations from references to a certain old pine or a radiating cluster of basswood trees.

We were generally accompanied on these expeditions by our dogs: Rocky, the womanizer, and Joe's yellow and white collie mix, Lady. They were good company, giving us the courage to explore a bit farther than we might have otherwise. The only downside was preventing them from scenting out and foolishly attacking a porcupine.

New sightings were always of great interest to us as well as to Dad. One early autumn afternoon Joe came running into our yard, out of breath with the news that Lady had treed a fisher down in John Longel's stand of pines. This formidable member of the weasel family was rare anywhere in the state at that time, extremely so in our part of south central Maine. Dad had never even seen one and was a little skeptical at first. But Joe's description seemed right, so we followed him, taking the shortest possible route. We soon came upon Lady, sitting at the base of a tree looking up, occasionally barking, her tail beating back and forth. It took a minute to sort out the creature amid the tangle of limbs, but once we did, we knew Joe was right. Peering down at us from a branch fifteen feet or so above was a sleek, dark-coated animal with a longish body, small round ears, and, because of his precarious situation, a bottle-brushed tail.

We hadn't been observing it for more than a few minutes when a movement not far away caught our attention and a second fisher loped into view, mustelid fashion. It quickly made its way up into the tree adjacent to the one in which its mate was confined by two yapping dogs and three ogling humans. We watched the pair for fifteen minutes or so, fascinated and feeling very privileged. Finally, we dragged off the dogs, who were already getting bored, and left the fishers in peace, with the hope they would establish a small population.

Dad's trapping days were winding down while I was still very young. He learned the hard way how to set for the uncannily elusive foxes, as well as for the more easily fooled raccoons and skunks. Before and during the war he made some much needed cash from his little trap line, but soon after, prices fell to a level where it was no longer worth bothering setting traps, even though it was a challenging endeavor Dad really enjoyed.

I do remember tangles of steel traps with their chains and grapples hanging from spikes at the back of the shed, and bluntly pointed pelt-stretching boards stacked at the top of the stairs leading under the barn. On a couple of these were old desiccated raccoon pelts, dry as parchment, with the hair falling out, that he had been unable to sell years before.

Dad subscribed to *Outdoor Life* and *Fur-Fish-Game* magazines, and I became enthralled by the photographs and stories about hunts for trophy Dall sheep, elk, cape buffalo, and, more realistically, white-tailed deer and black bear. Joe and I began thinking of ourselves as potential hunters and were given our first BB guns at pretty young ages. For the most part we used these air rifles to sharpen our eyes on inanimate objects such as bottles, tin cans, knotholes, and toadstools, but there was a brief period when, left to our own devices, we turned our air-powered rifles on ordinary songbirds and squirrels. For a few weeks one fall, the unused cow path leading down between wooded stone walls to the lower pasture became our hunting ground where we stalked and waited in ambush for whatever might come by. Thankfully, we were not very proficient with these BB guns, and our take was limited to a few sparrows, a cowbird, and a chipmunk. I don't know why Dad didn't just stop us before the senseless killing played out; perhaps because he had gone through a similar, much more deadly period of wasteful sport when at thirteen he had gotten his .22. I think both Joe and I realized this was wrong once we collected the lifeless and nearly weightless bundles of feathers, and we soon found more appropriate ways to spend our free time.

This isn't to say we'd lost our common interest in hunting. In fact, we were more enthused about it than ever, only now we were ready, at least in our own minds, to begin hunting legal game, in season and with real firearms. Joe's father, George, didn't hunt, but Joe received lots of advice and instruction from his uncle, Henry Davenport, and his cousin, Butch, as well as from Dad. Dad set some strict rules about handling firearms safely. We knew that if he ever caught either of us with a gun, loaded or otherwise, carelessly pointed in the direction of another person or a dwelling we wouldn't be out hunting again soon. I took over Dad's old single-shot .22 rifle, and George bought one for Joe. By now we were pouring over the pages of the sporting magazines with a new authority, gleaning every bit of information we could find, especially if written by *Outdoor Life*'s shooting editor, Jack O'Connor. We memorized the ballistics and shooting characteristics of calibers we would never have reason to use personally with our limited range of possibilities.

At fifteen Joe got a used 16-gauge single-shot shotgun, and Dad bought me a 20-gauge. We practiced with Dad on cans thrown up into the air until Joe bought a spring-loaded hand trap and we graduated to clay pigeons. This doesn't mean we shot a lot, maybe a couple boxes of shells total between the two of us. We then learned that shooting clay birds in the open had little resemblance to gunning for grouse in the October woods. These wary birds burst out of hiding with a heart-stopping clattering tattoo of wing beats, then twisted their way out through tangles of alders, witch hazel, and wild apple branches. Our delayed-reaction, poorly aimed shooting didn't discourage us in the least, and it's a lucky thing we weren't depending on those birds for our dinner.

At that time Maine was still facilitating a misguided pheasant-rearing program aimed at providing "game birds" other than our native grouse and migrating woodcock for wing shooters. These clueless birds, released a few weeks before the season opened, had no fear of humans and no natural escape behavior. Most were slaughtered as they stood watching the approaching hunters on the first day or two of the season. Worse yet, Maine's woodland-intensive habitat and its severe winters offered little chance for the few birds that did make it through the season to actually survive the winter and breed naturally the following spring. I managed to shoot a couple of these late-season pheasants when they showed up at the edge of the woods behind the barn, but didn't find it terribly satisfying. Meanwhile, Joe embarked upon a campaign to bag a crow—a very wary bird, then—but was experiencing little success. He claimed that crows knew a lot about firearm identification because whenever he went afield armed with his shotgun he'd encounter crows standing in a field or sitting on fence posts just out of range of his scattergun. But, when he carried his .22 rifle, he could find no crows offering themselves as sitting targets, but plenty flying slowly just overhead.

My real interest in hunting, boiled down to hunting deer—a challenging endeavor in our region, which at the time had a hunter success rate of around fifteen percent over a month-long season. From the time I turned ten, I'd been accompanying Dad on his pre-twilight hunts, lugging the .22 in case a rabbit or a fox offered itself up, although none ever did. I learned a lot about standing very still against a tree or sitting on a wall while watching a crossing or the edge of a field. And I knew what it was like to be so cold your teeth chattered and you shook like a paint shaker the entire way back home in the darkness. We sometimes saw deer, and I was with Dad when he missed one with his .30-30 Winchester. And I'd been present to share the exciting times when he'd brought a fresh-killed deer home.

My own chance came improbably on the final afternoon of the season, when I was twelve. Four days earlier, Dad had gotten a nice hundred-and-eighty-pound six-pointer along a well-used trail just a few hundred yards behind the barn. Now, as the final hour of the season began its countdown, we were standing up against a clump of birches watching that same run. This time, I was holding the .30-30. Just as I was about to shift into a less uncomfortable position, Dad put his hand on my shoulder and touched his ear. He'd heard the telltale crack of an approaching deer snapping a twig.

My eyes widened and I looked down at the rifle in my hands and began to shake. I'd never fired Dad's gun, but I had heard its bark and imagined it must kick like a mule. Soon, even over my shaking bones and wheezing breaths, I could hear the deer walking purposefully up the narrow passage between Longel's woodlot and the piece known as the Pile Place. Because of the birch trees, we wouldn't be able to see anything until it was practically abreast of us at close range. My shaking climbed to about a seven on the Richter scale, and I don't know whether the five-pointer was suicidal or merely deaf. Held to my shoulder, the rifle telegraphed my tremors, the muzzle describing erratic little loops. Four afternoons earlier, Dad's deer had stepped into sight just sixty feet away; now this buck was suddenly standing there only half that far away. I don't remember lining up the sights, jerking the trigger, or any percussion from the shot, but the bullet took the unlucky deer in the spine just ahead of the shoulder, and he literally dropped like a sack of bricks. An hour later we were walking up the path, guided by a flashlight beam, the deer being skidded easily along the frozen ground behind Don the draft horse.

Three years later on Christmas Day, I got my own .30-30, a used Winchester with a lot of character, and when I turned sixteen I was legally entitled to hunt alone. I learned a lot about hunting deer during those early years, and had a few chances, but I didn't shoot my next buck until I was seventeen. Joe got his first deer at that same age, but as I remember, he never was successful in his quest to bag a crow.

Fishing had never been a part of my father's life. He had neither the time nor the interest, but I developed an interest in the sport at an early age. North Auburn village, on Lake Auburn, was my favorite spot. In those days it had a real New England village flavor, with a white-clapboarded church, an active Grange, the Charles P. Wight School, and Lou Libby's general store. Lou was a friendly shopkeeper with wire-rimmed spectacles, bald on top with a graying fringe, and his signature apron. He kept a wheel of cheddar under a clear lid on the counter and sold groceries, candy, beer, cigarettes, ice cream, fishing tackle, and a little of almost anything. He also rented out aluminum boats. His store was bustling in the early spring with locals and with fishermen, many of them there to see if the white perch had started running. The cove at North Auburn was fed by the waters of the Basin, a former millpond that was reduced to a sluggish stream when the old dam went out one spring. In late April and early May, especially in the evening, this tributary attracted thousands of white perch, a silvery bass-like fish, prized by many for the excellent flavor of it fillets. In the village, two bridges crossed the inlet and it was on the lower one that a crowd of anglers jostled for position when the perch were in. Most tossed out bobbers with a worm-baited hook suspended a couple feet below. You usually didn't have long to wait before the bobber began dancing along the surface. When it was pulled under you set the hook and reeled in your perch. Inevitably, there were crossed lines and tangles, irritating to some of the serious meat fishermen, but for the most part the atmosphere was lighthearted, almost festive.

Most of the perch were six or seven inches long, but ten-inch perch weighing nearly a pound were not uncommon. Using dead smelts for bait, the Holbrook boys routinely took white perch up to two pounds, and occasionally larger. Once in a while, an angler rigged for perch would be surprised by a strike from a brown trout or brookie, or even a landlocked salmon. Far from being discouraged by the crazy, crowded conditions at North Auburn, this perch fishing actually whet my appetite and helped develop an appreciation for more solitary fishing adventures that were to come.

One such opportunity was afforded by Townsend Brook, which coursed along the eastern base of the hill on its way to Lake Auburn. Years before it had supported a small fish hatchery.

Although just a couple yards wide, Townsend Brook ran cold and deep beneath a shady canopy of interlaced branches. Small native trout thrived in the spring-fed book, lying beneath undercut banks, fallen trees, and in the deeper pools. One June day when we were ten or eleven, following directions from Butch Davenport, Joe and I walked the mile or so through our woodlot and down into the valley until our path intersected the stream. The water ran dark in the shadows, rippling on the surface, shot through with greenish gold light wherever struck by the dancing sunbeams.

We baited our lines with small worms and dropped them into likely looking holes, letting the current carry the bait down into the darkened lairs. Soon one of us would feel a sharp tug on the line as a small trout darted out and attacked the bait. More often than not we'd fail to hook the plucky little fish, but every so often out would come a twisting, gleaming jewel of a fish five or six inches long. Glistening in the sunlight these dark-flanked native brookies were perfect in every detail, from the mottled pattern on their dark green backs to the golden spots spattering their sides, white-rimmed fins of red, and their white bellies. We marveled at their beauty.

Only three trout caught that day measured the legal six inches, but one or two others, a bit shorter, were seriously injured by the hook, and since it was pointless to release them we added them to the catch. It seemed we'd only gotten started when we realized it was time to head back. Reluctantly we picked up our now-empty worm can, divided the trout and strung them on alder twigs, and, carrying our simple gear, started the walk back through the woods and up the hill to our homes.

My interest in fishing grew rapidly, my skills improving at a more moderate rate. Once I'd caught some good-sized pickerel at Sandy Bottom Pond I was no longer content with telescoping metal rods and single-action reels. I saved some money and purchased a new Mitchell open-faced spinning reel, along with a glass rod, an outfit with which you could cast a lure a country mile with no experience whatever. Relying on friends and relatives for transportation, Joe and I got to the Royal River for trout, and even to Rangeley and down to the coast at Fort Popham, hoping for stripers, but getting mostly mackerel and pollock.

Many new opportunities for widening my angling experiences arose once I purchased a beat-up Old Town canoe cast off by one of the summer camps. The deeply crazed canvas was painted red with a wide white stripe along the gunwales, and to me it was the fulfillment of a dream. I have to give my parents, avowed landlubbers, credit for being supportive of something they were obviously not pleased about.

*Things were looking up at the farm in 1964. The weather-beaten farmhouse had recently been given a facelift, which included taking off the two sagging porches. Linda had her blue-and-white Ford, I had purchased my canoe the year before, and Dad had his deer.*

Streams, rivers, and flowages previously unreachable were now accessible, and exploring them opened up whole new worlds. Using the canoe, my friend Harry Walker from North Auburn and I explored many inviting streams on Sundays in the spring, sometimes finding trout, other times coming up empty, but always discovering something of interest.

Eventually, I learned to handle a fly rod and fell under the spell of Hazen Poole, a fabulously accomplished fly fisherman who had won a number of state fly-casting tournaments back when there were such events, and had the elegant split bamboo rods he'd won to prove it. Hazen patiently taught me the basics of fly fishing and together we launched my canoe into nearby familiar waters and in others new to both of us. Hazen was a generous soul and a true gentleman. He loved fishing so much it interfered with his ability to stay with a steady job. It was always a great privilege to be out on the water with him and I only wish I'd done it more often.

Looking back, I believe the little ventures into the woods around Maple Hill Farm instilled in me a love and appreciation for things wild, for time spent out of doors, and a longing to explore the woods and waters of my own state and beyond. The cool, clear water flowing between rocks in the little brook in the back woodlot; the dancing sunlight, dappling the brown needles beneath John Longel's pines; the tiny speckled brook trout flashing below the surface in Townsend Brook—all imparted the same timeless message as the deep blue lakes in Maine's Allagash region, and the sparsely forested, windswept wilderness of Labrador. It's a message worth heeding, and a direction that has never steered me wrong.

# CHAPTER ELEVEN

## WINTER'S PROMISE KEPT

In winter there were no tomatoes to pick or weed, or any hay to get in, but by no means did this translate into less work to do around the place. For one thing, the cows were kept indoors and this meant they had to be fed. It also meant the manure needed to be cleaned out of their stalls twice each day. Because I had to go to school I was excused from this unglamorous job on mornings, but it was one of my chores, along with feeding the young stock, before supper.

Behind the cows' raised stalls and running the length of the tie-up was a two-foot-wide gutter about four inches deep. Each morning that gutter would be filled with steaming, soupy manure that had to be gotten rid of, and unlike

Hercules we had no nearby river to divert. It always amazed me how busy the cows must have been all night to provide such a prodigious quantity. The gutter was bordered by hinged wooden scuttles that were designed to be opened, making it relatively easy to scrape the manure to the opening with a hoe, and send it plummeting into the depths of the cavernous space below. As the winter dragged on, even this enormous void would become filled with huge mounds of this composting material that grew like stalagmites up to the scuttles.

Occasionally Dad would go below and clear away some of the manure, but even in years when all this natural fertilizer had been removed and spread on the fields, the shallow end of the huge cellar would be filled to capacity. This meant that ever-longer stretches of the gutter had to be cleared by shoving a steel grain shovel along its length until you reached the first opening that still had space below. To accomplish this you needed to be physically in the gutter up against the cows' tail ends, which provided them an ideal opportunity to swat you square in the face with a tail coated in the soupy mixture. Once the stalls and gutter were cleaned (we never called it "mucking out") we spread sawdust or shavings under the animals for a dry bed.

To produce this quantity of manure, the cows needed to eat at least an equal volume in hay, plus drink an enormous amount of water, since they were each also producing twenty-five or so quarts of milk. The watering part was not difficult because the cow barn was equipped with on-demand drinking cups, each shared by two adjacent cows. A wide, flat disk inside the steel bowl permitted water to flow in when depressed by the cow's nose. Even new cows learned the process almost instantly, and the only flaw in the design was a tendency of the valves to sometimes stick in the open position spilling water over the rim. Most of this overflow simply ran into the boxlike manger at each cow's head, then trickled or poured down below through cracks in the wood. But it was a waste of water we could ill afford with two families and forty-five large animals depending upon a shallow spring-fed well a quarter-mile away across a snow-covered field.

Each afternoon at around four, Dad grained the milkers, while I cleaned out the barn. After supper, while Dad milked, I'd water the young stock and the horses, none of which had automatic drinking cups. Then I'd climb up into the mows, or even the scaffolds, and throw down onto the hay barn floor enough bales to feed everyone. While the cow barn kept a pretty mild temperature due to its low ceilings and the concentration of body heat in the somewhat confined space, the cavernous hay barn had no such furnace and was not much warmer than the outdoors. It also was very poorly lighted; in fact, just three defiant little light bulbs mounted beneath the fifteen-foot-high scaffolds were charged with beating back the darkness in the entire space. Very little light made it into the hay-filled mows, and less still up into the scaffolds. As I pulled down bales from their stacked tiers, carried them to the mow's edge, and tossed them down to the floor, my imagination kept speculating as to just what variety of horror, escaped from the grave, or homicidal maniac crouched, hidden in the hay that night waiting to reach out and grab me. So convincing would these images become, that I would be close to a state of full blown panic by the time I hurriedly tossed down the final bale. Often eschewing the ladder, I'd simply swing down from the eight-foot mow and land with a thud on the floor below.

Once safe in the dimly lighted bay, I'd get a hold of myself, and the grisly images would melt away. With forced composure I'd push open the door to the warm, relatively well-lighted cow barn and nonchalantly walk in.

Another little chore of winter was filling the kitchen wood box, usually accomplished by lugging a couple armloads of split firewood up the back stairs from the woodshed. But there were a couple years when my folks decided that kerosene for the parlor heater was too expensive and, as a result, an additional woodstove, a tall Round Oak with chrome trim and a figurine on the top, had to be provided for. Its appetite for firewood was tremendous and together the two wood boxes required more than a few trips up and down the creaky stairs.

The two stoves did an adequate job heating our apartment during the day and in the evening while they were stoked and burning, but it was a different matter as the night dragged on and the fires dwindled while outside the mercury plummeted and the north wind strengthened. By morning, without the lovely, even heat of the oil burner, the house and particularly our bedrooms would be quite nippy. The thick frost tracery that had formed on the windows, although beautiful in its own way, was not especially cheery when you had to get out of your warm bed and put your feet down on the icy floor. Earlier you heard Dad rattling the lids on the kitchen stove, and presently the reassuring sounds of kindling snapping and popping. With the fire started, the kitchen warmed up reasonably quickly, but if the night had been cold enough, it was probably too late to have prevented the water pipes that led up along the uninsulated north wall from freezing. If the wind continued to blow, there was no way Dad could start the fires without at least a little smoke escaping into the rooms. This gave rise to a rather sarcastic phrase of mine, which hopefully added a bit of dark humor to the morning situation.

"Oh boy!" I'd chirp, sitting up in bed and taking a deep breath. "My favorite kind of morning: cold and smoky." Instead of giving me what I probably deserved, Mother and Dad again retained their basic good natures, letting the comment pass in its intended spirit.

Of course winter also provided some opportunities for fun as well. With snow on the ground from late November to mid-March, there was always a chance for an unseasonable warm spell with a little rain, followed by a hard freeze. These conditions could result in a half-inch-thick crust on top of the snow, creating ideal conditions for our steel-runnered Lightning Glider sleds. Everything ran downhill from our place, so with proper crust you could fly down any number of great hills, lying on your belly on the sled. The steering system, although not great, generally allowed you to veer off enough at the bottom to avoid colliding head-on into the trees, stone walls, and barbed-wire fences that rimmed the edge of every field. It was a different story with Butch Davenport's toboggan. You didn't need perfect crust with the toboggan's wide, flat wooden bottom, so long as you were willing to first pack a trail. But with no real steering the only option at the bottom to avoid a serious pile-up was for everyone to bail off before the hurtling missile struck something solid.

Everyone's dog naturally came along for the fun, running down alongside and often directly in front of the sleds, causing additional mid-hill collisions, usually not serious in nature. By the tail end of the afternoon our canine friends would be exhausted, and mostly watched the last few runs, lying in the snow at the top of the hill.

Some of the things we enjoyed in winter were not necessarily considered winter activities. Horseback riding was one of them; not on the worst winter days, but on sunny days in late February and March a short ride was a good antidote for cabin fever. It all started when Marilyn Davenport got Fury, her pinto saddle horse, and we all learned to ride. Fury was western-reined and pretty dependable, and we all learned to ride, as best we could, without formal instruction or supervision. Before long everybody was getting a horse, including the three Hardy kids from the farm on the other side of the hill; our friends from North Auburn, Harry and Jean Walker; and eventually even Linda and me.

Late one winter Dad got a bargain on a little bay gelding from Brunswick with a black mane and tail and white stockings. Linda named him Star for a little white patch in the middle of his forehead. Star loved to run, which we found out the first time Linda tried him out on just such a warm February afternoon. As soon as Dad let go of the bridle, Star—with Linda in the saddle—wheeled around and galloped down the driveway, past the snow banks,

*My sister, Linda, with Star, her saddle horse. Star had lots of spirit, even though he suffered from an asthma-type condition known as the heaves.*

and onto the road. Without slowing a bit he turned right and proceeded at a full gallop down what to him was an unfamiliar road. Linda was unable to check his speed, but fortunately there was no traffic and the ice along the side of the road had turned to slush in the warm sunshine. Mother was beside herself as might be imagined, and Dad made for the car, thinking to follow. The rest of us stared after them slack-jawed, wondering if we'd ever see either Linda or Star again.

*Here, Linda leads Star in 1961, with one of the neighbor kids, Joleen Walker, taking a ride.*

As horse and rider approached the first steeply sloped section of road where disaster was almost inevitable, Joe's grandmother, seventy-something-year-old Lizzie Tomlinson, on her way to the mailbox, heard Linda's yells. Looking up she saw this wild apparition bearing down on her and she made an instantaneous and courageous decision to step out in front of them and wave her arms. The road being narrow because of the snow banks on either side caused Star to stop rather than veer around Mrs. Tomlinson, who grabbed hold of the bridle.

*The one-horse "pung" sleigh was the pickup truck of the nineteenth century. Here, Dad gives some friends a turn around the fields in 1962 with Black Beauty in the traces.*

Rather than dismounting, Linda caught her breath, thanked this brave lady, turned Star back toward the farm, and again he took off at a full gallop. "Look," someone in the yard yelled. "She's coming back!" Linda reined Star into the driveway and Dad stopped them short before Star ran into the low-clearanced shed door, which would have mowed Linda off like Wile E. Coyote at a railroad tunnel.

After that introduction we learned to keep a tight rein on Star, and he turned into a nice little horse. We learned that for all his spirit he suffered from an asthma-like condition called heaves, but he did well as long as we kept him off dusty hay.

Our second saddle horse, Black Beauty, was a large mare, seemingly in perfect health, and just about the opposite of Star in spirit and energy. It turned out that Black Beauty had been trained to pull, as well as for the saddle, and Dad got a deal on an old wooden sleigh called a pung. When the snow in the field across the road wasn't too deep, Dad would hitch her up and take friends for rides. The pung's two seats could hold four adults plus a few bags or boxes of supplies in the bed behind.

One twenty-first of February—Linda's birthday—a gibbous moon was shining brightly over the snowy fields that glittered as though dusted with diamonds. There being a bit of packed snow left on the road by the snowplow,

Dad hitched Black Beauty up to the pung for an evening sleigh ride "around the square." I was at an age where I felt a little weird participating in this type of activity, especially if it had been in broad daylight. But I was glad for once I hadn't let my fear of appearing uncool interfere with another nice experience. It was an almost magical ride, the four of us bundled up against the cold, Black Beauty's condensed breath blossoming in the moonlight, and her harness bells singing out a carol as she clip-clopped along the quiet roads beneath the bare trees that cast long purple shadows across our path. It was a special birthday treat for all of us, and one we'd never forget.

Christmas was a big deal in our family, and it wasn't diminished by the fact that we didn't have unlimited funds to buy the most expensive gifts for each other. We would select the least scraggly and uneven tree from our woodlot, which was never known for its production of balsam firs, saw it down, and drag it home where we decorated it in the best tradition of the forties and fifties. This included the rather large colored lights widely spaced along the cord—the kind that if one bulb went bad the entire string would quit. The glass balls and ornaments were placed on the tree according to size.

Small ones near the top, large ones along the bottom—
that was the law. The hanging of the tinsel was another big
issue; this was the heavy metallic tinsel and not the cheap
cellophane "icicles." Dad insisted the strands be applied
individually and hung evenly without so much as a single
strand resting an end on a lower branch. This usually resulted
in Dad ending up doing most of the job himself. I must
admit, however, his efforts did pay off, making a beautiful tree
out of one that appeared to have limited prospects.

Christmas morning was spent at home, and after chores
Linda and I, long past believing in Santa, first emptied the
stockings we'd hung Christmas Eve, which resembled nothing
so much as a witch's support hose or a python that had just
swallowed some piglets. We were always delighted by the
small toys and surprises we found in the stockings, nearly as
much so as by the larger gifts waiting for us beneath the tree.
Mother and Dad always had something for each other as
well, and Linda and I stretched what little money we'd saved
to buy something for our folks as well as for each other. These
gifts didn't amount to much, and I remember one year, when
I was eight or nine, thinking Dad was really going to love the
key chain with the little shrunken alligator head.

At noon we'd drive over to my grandparents' in Lewiston,
there joining Mother's sister, Stephanie, her husband, Frank,
and their boys, Tom and Dan. There Babci would serve drinks

and all manner of treats before we'd open more presents and eventually sit down to one of her sumptuous Polish-flavored Christmas dinners.

One rather lean December all the preparations were made as usual. The tree was up and the presents wrapped; although we all knew things would be scaled down a bit that year.

Then, with just the weekend to wait until Christmas, Dad got a call. It was Ken Smith, a small logging contractor for whom Dad sometimes found woodlots. They'd been working on a deal with a landowner in Sabattus that had been stalled since fall. Now, all of a sudden, the transaction was back on track and Ken wanted Dad to estimate the stumpage on a small parcel that had been added to the pot before closing the deal. Although it was Saturday and snowing lightly, we drove out for a look at the timber on this small piece. It didn't take long for Dad to determine the volume of wood was clearly present. Smith could close the deal and it would mean a couple thousand dollars for Dad in a few weeks—a big boost at the time.

We drove back through Lewiston in the accumulating snow. It was within an hour of closing time for most of the stores and they would not be open on Sunday. Dad pulled up beside the P. B. Peck department store. Because of the snowstorm even the last-minute shopping crowd was light.

We went right up the stairs to the women's department and Dad knew exactly the dress Mother wanted for New Year's Eve but was not expecting. He used a little metal charge plate to pay for it, knowing he could afford it once he got his commission for the woodlot.

Our next stop, just minutes before they closed, was at a nice little gift shop in Auburn. In the growing darkness with snow floating down, the little shop with a warm light showing through the small panes looked exactly like a painting on a Christmas card. Inside Dad bought a horse figurine Linda had been coveting, along with a few smaller ones for her stocking. Finally, we stopped just down the street at Eithe's Bakery and picked up a box of their flakey cream horns filled with real whipped cream. Then we got back in the car and headed around the lake for home. We'd be a little late starting chores, but we had some good news to share.

# CHAPTER TWELVE

## SPRING'S FICKLE DANCE

The trouble with spring is the tentative way in which it arrives. After months of drifting snow, howling winds, slippery footing, and frozen pipes, we were ready for spring to come charging in and roust out Old Man Winter, who seemed determined to maintain his icy grip on the frozen countryside. A pair of wonderfully warm, sunny days could be followed by ten inches of snow falling the next. On its tail would be a relentless northwest wind, clearing out the storm and replacing it with temperatures not much different from those of January. Next might come a thaw, but with it a cold, clammy drizzle coating everything with a film of moisture that during the next night would freeze solid.

By March the firewood supply would be nearly exhausted, even though we still needed a reliable heat source for another six weeks, and evening fires to take off the chill a month beyond that. If Dad and Gran'pa had been working in the woods over the winter, it was still possible to bring out a load or two of wood on the scoot early in the morning after a freezing night. This would likely be a mix of softwood, hardwood limbs, and smallish tree sections, most of it green—the kind of firewood that sizzled rather than crackled in the stove once it finally got started, and gave off little heat.

After the horses were gone and work in the woods stopped, we'd end up buying a few cords of firewood. Often this would be from unreliable providers whose measure would be short or whose mix leaned heavily to gray birch, soft maple, and even poplar.

Even more serious would be a shortage of hay. As the herd gradually grew once Dad took over the farm, the cows frequently outstripped the supply of hay put up the summer before. This led to the self-defeating practice of buying additional hay in the early spring when the prices were premium and the quality of the hay less than perfect. Still, it was that or sell off livestock that, before long, could be turned out to pasture, where excellent forage would be plentiful and essentially no work on our part required.

Purchasing hay often put the farm finances just enough behind so that it would take the entire summer's efforts to catch up—when we were lucky.

But springtime also had its benefits and was eagerly anticipated. The first sunny days warm enough to melt back the snow around the bases of trees on the southern exposures would start small trickles of water running down along the roadsides. These would generally refreeze during the night, but eventually these little rivers would swell in volume, and tripping along their slushy banks, they begged to be dammed up. And that's exactly what Henry and I would do when we got off the bus after school.

Wearing green rubber boots we'd head for the roadside armed with a shovel and a hoe, and launch into building a series of slush dams along the edge of our front yard. The magic was in the rushing, roily green water itself, and the point was to allow its passage through an outlet at each dam into the reservoir below. If we allowed the dams to get too deep, say above eight inches, the backed-up water would spread out across the road, annoying the infrequent drivers who passed by; Dad would then instruct us to breach our handiwork and allow the water to escape.

This we would do on our own in any event, once we grew tired of our engineering or became soaked through with the icy melt water. Having few toy boats of the right scale we'd content ourselves with chips of wood to represent rafts or canoes running down with the current.

Maple Hill was aptly named because of the abundance of sugar maples, both in the woodlots and along stretches of road. This was especially true between our farm and the Longels', as well as in our yard, which supported several mature trees with heavy spreading limbs and healthy crowns. These regal maples were perfect for a syrup operation, but that was yet another seasonal venture that we never had the time or energy to take full advantage of.

After the winter dormancy, the sugar-rich sap stored in the tree's roots over the winter begins to rise up into the tree once daytime temperatures climb high enough—a few degrees above freezing for several days. These conditions can arise as early as late February, but on average the prime sap-running season encompasses two or three weeks in March. During the season, this lifeblood of the tree rises up inside the bundles of hollow phloem located just beneath the rough bark, on its way to each branching twig in the tree's crown where it will nourish an awakening bud. When the nighttime temperature drops below freezing the internal pressure is eased and some of this sap flows back down into the roots, only to be sent back up the next warm day. It is this pumping action that accounts for the relatively long sapping season, when the sweet, slightly sticky fluid can be interrupted during its passage and diverted into receptacles, or in the case of big operations, hose networks. Metal or plastic spiles are inserted into the cambium of the tree and, at least in the days of my youth, buckets, cans, or jugs hung beneath the spiles to catch the steady drips of sap.

Although most years we tapped a tree or two just for this sweet tonic, there was one season when we went at it a bit more seriously. On a day selected for its warm temperatures, Dad would drill into the furrowed gray bark with an auger bit in a brace, angling the hole slightly upward. Two or so inches of penetration was sufficient, and the clumpy sawdust, wet with sap and extruded by the auger, was an indicator that the season had indeed started. Lacking genuine sap buckets, which are tall and narrow and equipped with lids to keep out snow and rain, we used a variety of collection containers, including a few two-quart mason jars.

When there was a strong flow of sap these needed to be emptied two or more times during the day, and if Dad was too busy and we kids were at school, Mother would empty the contents into a bucket and add the take to the variety of pots and pans on the wood end-heater on the kitchen range, where the refining began. This reduction process required a significant amount of energy to complete, when you consider the ratio of raw sap to finished syrup runs about forty to one.

With the sap bubbling slowly on the stovetop pans, the kitchen would fill with a lovely sweet aroma. Partially reduced sap would be combined with similar batches to be reduced still further, and in the evening Dad might finish up a batch in a pan on one of the range's propane burners for added control. The results of this great maple syrup venture were a few quarts of delicious but commercially imperfect syrup, and the walls adjacent to the stove stripped clean of their wallpaper by the rising steam.

But it was the maple sap itself that we really loved and continued collecting in small quantities. It was a treat to go outside and lift a frosty jar of nearly frozen sap from a spile and enjoy a deep draft of this distinctive life-affirming tonic. It is the taste of springtime itself, and if not a proven elixir, it's the best medicine I know to cleanse the bitter taste of winter from one's palette and spirit.

Once February was out of the way, we eagerly kept our eyes open for the traditional and natural harbingers of spring. The first sighting of a returning robin was one hallmark that instilled an inflated sense of accomplishment in the observer, and even the appearance of red-winged black-birds and starlings was a cause for excitement. And of course the first wedge of geese honking overhead brought us out for a look as quickly as that first retreating flock heard the previous October.

I don't recall any crocuses in the flower plots around the house, but the first signs of tulips and daffodils breaking the surface, even before all the snow had melted, was taken as another affirmation of good things to come.

Best of all were the choruses of the spring peepers that filled the air around boggy areas big and small during the latter part of April. On our well-drained hill there were few low, wet spots that attracted concentrations of these highly vocal little tree frogs, so Dad would drive us down along the marshy inlet of the lake two or three evenings during the season, where the volume of the peepers' mating chorus swelled to a level that was almost too rich and sweet to bear.

Once I'd been bitten by the fishing bug, the approach of springtime took on a whole new meaning. Primed and psyched by the fishing stories that had been monopolizing the pages of the sporting magazines since February, I would be ridden with anxiety, contemplating whether or not there would be actual open water for the April 1 start of the season. The best bet was usually the inlet where Townsend Brook entered Lake Auburn through a culvert under Lake Shore Drive. There, the current would begin wearing a small crescent of open water in the still solid ice around the Ides of March. Some years this opening would be as wide as fifty feet and extend out into the lake a hundred feet or more. Other opening days there would be only a little patch of water twenty feet long and half that wide, providing little opportunity to cast a lure or a streamer fly. Not that it was a big deal, because the water temperature was still too cold for much chance at a fish anyway. But that wouldn't stop me from getting down there at every opportunity to stand freezing, alongside a few other numb stiffs, throwing our offerings squarely into a frigid headwind, our wet, red hands numbing to the point we could barely operate our reels. Finally, around mid-April, the swelling ranks of fishermen would begin picking up an occasional salmon or trout, but more frequently a pickerel or nothing at all.

By the time I became involved, the once-generous seasons for dipping smelt in the spring were coming to a close. Biologists were discovering just how crucial these prolific and very tasty little fish were to the health of the trout and salmon fisheries. As limits were reduced and evermore streams were closed to the taking of this early spring spawner that ascended the lake tributaries under the darkness of night, another colorful Maine tradition was passing from the scene, albeit for good reasons.

*Here I am, rowing "Sandy" on Sandy Bottom Pond, on my way to try outwitting a pickerel in 1963. Our little lot and camp on this nearby pond provided an easy-to-get-to escape from the endless chores that were always waiting around the farm.*

One late April when I was in high school, Harry Walker, one of my grownup hunting and fishing buddies, received a tip that the smelt were running in a little tributary of Anasagunticook Lake in nearby Canton and that dipping them was permitted, although the daily limit was reduced to two quarts of the silvery little fish, down from eight quarts a few years before. This earlier bag limit sounds overly generous, but there was a time when the smelt population was considered inexhaustible and dippers would fill up an eight-quart pail with just two swipes of the net into water black with the teeming fish.

We arrived at the dirt road leading down to the lake after dark, and it was immediately apparent that this secret was not well-kept. Vehicles lined both sides of the road with fishermen coming and going between the brook and the road and gathering in knots, where they smoked, drank beer, and obviously swapped yarns. Always the serious sportsmen, Harry and I wove our way around these groups and, guided by a flashlight, worked our way down to the stream bank. The short section of stream appeared alive with bobbing lights, and we caught snatches of conversations as well as salty expletives when someone stepped over his boots or caught his long handled net in the brush. We followed the stream down to the lakeshore without coming across a likely spot to try our luck. The night was growing cold, and in the starlight you could see fifty yards out from shore a pan of lingering ice that probably still covered most of the lake. A widening shroud of fog was just beginning to obscure this sight, and from the mist and the darkness you could hear mewing seagulls apparently roosting on the ice pan.

We headed back up along the stream and the evidence was the same everywhere: very few fishermen were dipping any fish. A flashlight beam directed into the stream reached clear to the sandy gravel bottom, when in good times the light would be interrupted by a solid phalanx of dark dorsal surfaces of urgently ascending smelt. We stood back to take in the carnival-like atmosphere—most of the fishermen didn't seem to mind the scarcity of fish. I didn't smoke, but Harry lit his pipe.

On one bend in the stream a couple guys were netting a few smelt—four or five at a time, working toward their two-quart limits. Someone tapped Harry on the shoulder— a stranger, the whites of his eyes glowing from his darkened face in the uncertain light. He nodded toward his pail then led us to the spot where he'd filled his modest limit. His light revealed nothing at first, but if you paid attention you'd catch glimpses of an occasional smelt darting across the gravel to the deeper shelter beneath the undercut bank.

We thanked him and took turns standing over the little run, careful not to shine the light down and spook the fish.

We didn't even need to wade in the water, which was a good thing since I discovered earlier that evening that one of my hip boots leaked.

In about an hour and a half we'd dipped our four quarts, the last pint or two coming very slowly. Most of the crowd had left but there were still a few stragglers gathered around the remaining cars, talking and laughing.

We both realized how cold we'd become, especially our hands and my one wet foot. We placed the half-bucket of fish along with the fine-meshed net into the back of Harry's Jeep and climbed in. Dipped in egg, then rolled in crumbs and fried in butter, those smelt were going to taste awfully good.

And so the seasons changed at Maple Hill Farm, each distinctive, each as familiar as an old friend, yet always imparting a sense of renewal. As each season approached we held our own expectations, which were sometimes met and sometimes not. Often, they held their own surprises, some more welcome than others. On the farm we geared our lives according to their rhythm, and they still serve as guideposts to my most vivid memories of growing up on Maple Hill Farm.

# Afterword

When I went off to the University of Maine in 1966, Dad made the wise decision to sell the dairy cows and replace them with beef cattle. This eliminated twice-daily milking, 365 days a year, and the young stock could stay with their mothers outside in the pasture all summer and fall. Then they could either be sold or kept over the winter for another cycle. It was an easy conversion with the existing pastures and fields and, of course, the barn and haying equipment in place. And there was a whole lineup of Mackenzie boys up the road eager to help with the haying. The white-faced Herefords did well on the farm's rich land and lent at least an air of prosperity to the place. Dad, although not exactly a gentleman farmer now, had a little more time to enjoy life.

*After I went off to college, Dad converted the herd from dairy cows to beef cattle, raising primarily polled Herefords. Not requiring milking, the beef critters were easier to care for, and the calves got to spend their early lives out in the pasture with their mothers. For years they were attended by Dad's donkey, Applejack, who took seriously his role as herd mascot and guardian.*

He continued raising tomatoes, a couple thousand plants, and Heather the Old English sheepdog produced a healthy and valuable litter of puppies each year, although Mother was finding it increasingly difficult to send the puppies off to unknown homes. Within a few years she retired Heather from the kennel business and began working falls and winters in an apple-packing plant at a large orchard across the lake on Perkins Ridge. Mother had remained at home, providing an immaculate, warm, and welcoming home all the time we kids were growing up, and now she enjoyed the chance to get out, earn her own spending money, and interact with the other women at this laid-back workplace.

Gran'pa Vincent died at age eighty while I was at college, and Babci and Dzidzu Klimek, as well as Aunt Annie, passed away while I was in the Navy in Rhode Island with my wife, Debbie, and our first child, David.

During that period Dad sold the fields and woods across the road to an Auburn businessman who continued to let Dad use the land as his own for, as it turned out, the rest of his life. With the money, my parents were able to do a major conversion of the farmhouse and after thirty years of living on the second floor, moved into the first floor apartment, which had been remodeled to reveal the hand-hewn beams and wide pumpkin pine floor boards of the original pre-1800s cape. Aunt Lydia relocated to the upstairs apartment.

Although working in town, Linda had continued to live on the farm, until 1981 when her new husband, Les Bickford, built for them a new house in the field above the orchard. A year or two later, they presented Dad with Applejack the donkey. Applejack immediately assumed the duty of herd guardian, showing no fear when he placed himself squarely between his cows and a curious bull moose twice his size. Another time he "protected" them from a bull my father had borrowed for breeding the cows, by breaking its leg with a well-placed kick. The bull needed to be destroyed and Dad had to compensate the owner. But even this didn't sour Dad on his beloved donkey. Other interesting creatures came to take the place of those before them, including a chicken that lived for twenty-one years. Each summer afternoon at around four, the Rhode Island red biddy would announce itself at the kitchen screen door. It stood there, head cocked, peering inside until my mother came to the door and gave her an Oreo cookie. Then there were the white domestic ducks abandoned at the lake by summer residents and rescued at freeze-up at great peril to Dad and some of the neighbors. And of course Sammy Lamb, the "lamb chop dinner" that ended up staying around until he died of old age at thirteen. But these are all stories for another time.

Gradually, other parcels of the farm were sold, as Maple Hill completed its transition from a rural farming community to a high-end residential neighborhood. Applejack died in March 1998, while Dad was hospitalized with complications from surgery. The fall before, Mrs. Mooley, the last of the Herefords had been sold, and Maple Hill Farm was left for the first time without farm animals.

Dad had the good fortune of living with Mother on the farm he loved and had moved to at the age of three months right up until his death at eighty in October 2005.